SUPER*naturally*
True

A Collection of Uplifting
Spiritual Encounters

First published by O Books, 2009
O Books is an imprint of John Hunt Publishing Ltd., The Bothy, Deershot Lodge, Park Lane, Ropley,
Hants, SO24 0BE, UK
office1@o-books.net
www.o-books.net

Distribution in:	South Africa
	Alternative Books
UK and Europe	altbook@peterhyde.co.za
Orca Book Services	Tel: 021 555 4027 Fax: 021 447 1430
orders@orcabookservices.co.uk	
Tel: 01202 665432 Fax: 01202 666219	Text copyright Jenny Smedley 2008
Int. code (44)	
	Design: Stuart Davies
USA and Canada	
NBN	ISBN: 978 1 84694 231 0
custserv@nbnbooks.com	
Tel: 1 800 462 6420 Fax: 1 800 338 4550	All rights reserved. Except for brief quotations
	in critical articles or reviews, no part of this
Australia and New Zealand	book may be reproduced in any manner without
Brumby Books	prior written permission from the publishers.
sales@brumbybooks.com.au	
Tel: 61 3 9761 5535 Fax: 61 3 9761 7095	The rights of Jenny Smedley as author have
	been asserted in accordance with the
Far East (offices in Singapore, Thailand,	Copyright, Designs and Patents Act 1988.
Hong Kong, Taiwan)	
Pansing Distribution Pte Ltd	
kemal@pansing.com	A CIP catalogue record for this book is available
Tel: 65 6319 9939 Fax: 65 6462 5761	from the British Library.

Printed by Digital Book Print

SUPER*naturally* True

A Collection of Uplifting Spiritual Encounters

Jenny Smedley

BOOKS

Winchester, UK
Washington, USA

CONTENTS

Acknowledgements

I'd like to thank **Mary Bryce**, the editor of *Chat, it's fate*
magazine, and very probably the nicest editor in the world,
for her help with this book, and with my writing in general.

I'd like to thank **Belinda Wallis**, editor of Take 5 magazine in
Australia, without whom I would not be where I am today.

I'd like to thank *John Hunt of O Books*,
without whom there would be no books.

Miracles, in the sense of phenomena we cannot explain, surround us on every hand: life itself is the miracle of miracles.
George Bernard Shaw

Miracles are not contrary to nature, but only contrary to what we know about nature.
St. Augustine

Miracles happen to those who believe in them.
Bernard Berenson

Introduction

How differently would you view your life, if you knew for certain that death wasn't the end? How would it change you and the way you saw the world if you knew that it all had meaning, difficult though it is to see it sometimes?

If you'd talked to loved ones who had passed over, and if you'd had spiritual encounters, proving to you that life after death was a fact, you'd live your life in a very different, much more optimistic way.

The people that have contributed to this book know these things, they have seen spirits, heard spirits and communicated with spirits, and they know that life after death is a reality for us all. Here they offer to share that knowledge and their experiences with you.

I'm sure you've seen many books out there on the 'supernatural' that are designed to chill the senses and freeze the bones. But, as I've discovered on my voyage through life, the majority of supernatural stories are actually uplifting and inspirational. This book is dedicated to the nicer kind, the kind of supernatural experience that seems like a miracle when it happens.

I've had many experiences myself throughout my life so far, that have proven to me over and over again that there is more to the human race than merely the physical. When my Dad was dying I actually saw his spirit body leaving his physical one. It gave a very sad situation an overtone of joyfulness. I was able to accept that my father had truly shaken off his disease-ridden body, and gone on to a new and miraculous life in another realm. I'd still lost my Dad, in that I would never hug his physical body again, but I knew that somewhere he still existed, and wasn't in pain, and that was a huge comfort to me.

When I lost my Mum, she manifested to me in many strange

ways, not least of which was through a shooting star that appeared in the sky exactly as I asked for a sign from her. I've had readings from mediums, who have been able to name my Mum and my Dad, but not only that – they have also named my Dad's brothers and two of his friends who are also in spirit, and whose names I didn't even recognize at first.

Animals too have manifested to me. Our dog, Ace, not only came back as a spirit presence to assure us that all was well with her, but she eventually came back in another body, complete with amazing physical evidence that she was the same dog we'd previously lost (see *Forever Faithful* – O Books).

Life after death and visits from beyond are rarely anything to be afraid of. On the following pages you'll read about angelic intervention, long lost loved ones coming back with vital messages, supernatural dreams, and examples of the myriad and bizarre ways that spirits often choose to communicate with us, people close to them who are still slogging our way through our physical life. I've come across so many truly wonderful stories that I wanted to put together a collection of the best ones in book form, especially for those days when you might be feeling a little lost and alone in the Universe. One thing is certain to me…none of us are alone.

Not everyone will relate to these experiences, not being ready to believe what they haven't seen with their own eyes, and that's how it's meant to be. If everyone in the world suddenly had total faith that death wasn't the end, that shock would be even greater for man than if little green men suddenly landed in front of The White House, and asked to be 'taken to our leader'!

If everyone suddenly believed in life after death, not just as a sop to religion, but really, genuinely, believed it, then the world would be in chaos.

Spiritual enlightenment is meant to be a gradual thing, and so, if you are someone who dismisses the stories that follow, than that's just the way you're meant to be, for now. If you're someone whose life is changed and whose spirit is uplifted by this book, then you're ready for the wonderful changes that will come to the *whole* of the world, in good time.

The communal soul of the Earth is ready to achieve critical mass, so don't despair if you are one of the 'converted' already. Once enough people have had their spiritual switch clicked to 'on' then mass knowing will overcome skepticism and every living person on the planet will also be switched on. As more and more spiritual seed-planters start spreading their messages of joy around the globe, the faster this evolutionary change will occur.

Chapter One

The Power of Loved Ones

Nothing prepares you for the loss of a loved one. Whether their going is sudden or agonizingly slow, the shock is terrible. Most people's first reaction after the disbelief has faded is a dreadful need to know that their loved ones still exist and are safe in another place.

I'm delighted to be able to bring you stories that will free you from that fear should you ever have to face this situation. This is probably the longest chapter in the book because of course loved ones are the ones we miss most, and they're the ones who strive the hardest to send through a sign or a manifestation to bring comfort to those of us they left behind.

It's not always easy for spirits to connect with the living world. I've heard it likened to trying to tune in a dodgy radio to an indistinct and fuzzy signal. Nevertheless, love does find a way.

I've heard people say that the worst part of learning to live again after losing a loved one is that every day survived from that moment, is a day that takes the bereaved further away from that person.

I hope after reading the stories in this chapter, you'll come to understand that we never leave anyone behind when we move forward in life, because they are always moving forward with us.

*

The Ballerina in the Snow

Jill Prior

When you get a phone call like the one we got in February 1991, your whole world slips away from you and leaves you spinning in an empty void. When it came to us, my husband Roger and I, both fell into shock and disbelief.

Our daughter, Lisa, had always wanted to be a ballerina and had never considered doing anything else. She didn't have the opportunity to take up ballet until she was eleven years old, which is quite late, but she proved to be so talented that despite everything, at the age of eighteen she was accepted by the Central School of Ballet in London.

As her parents we were thrilled for her. Certain of the path her life would take, Lisa moved away from home into a room in a house filled with like-minded, artistic people, and she was very happy. Her life was filled with promise and an amazing career beckoned. However, when she was twenty, tragedy struck. She injured her back, and was told by doctors that a grueling career as a ballerina was out of the question.

As far as Lisa was concerned, her life was over. She could see no way forward, but the Central School of Ballet didn't want to entirely lose someone so talented, so they tried to persuade her to change course and become a teacher for them. She refused to listen, because for her it was being a dancer or nothing.

She came home, and we had a terrible few months with her as she struggled to come to terms with her dream dying.

Thank goodness she was very strong and finally she started to see reason, accepting that to teach dance had merits after all, and was a way to stay in touch with the world she loved. She was accepted at teacher training college, passed her exams with flying colors, and moved back to the house in London to take up her post as teacher at the ballet school. The children adored her, and before long we had our happy daughter back, as she came to understand how much a teacher can give.

On February 10th 1991, Roger and I were excited as Lisa was going to be coming home for half-term. We loved her visits because her energy and enthusiasm lifted the whole house, filling it with light and passion, and after she'd gone it was like being in the aftermath of a whirlwind. Everything would become extra quiet.

It was snowing in Yorkshire, where we lived, we knew that it was snowing even more heavily in London, but we had no doubt she'd make it home.

Then we got the phone call that destroyed us.

I answered the phone, but Roger had to take it from me as I staggered around the kitchen, barely able to breathe, crying, "No, no!"

I had been told that Lisa was dead, our daughter, so full of life, who I was expecting to walk through the front door, was never, ever, coming home again. My mind could not accept it. The words made no sense to me at all.

We were told that snow had blocked the boiler flue in the house in London, and no-one had realized that the odorless but poisonous carbon monoxide gas had been piped straight into the bathroom because it couldn't escape into the open air. Being a health fanatic, Lisa was always up early to go for a run, so she was first into the bathroom. She was dead within ten minutes. Carbon monoxide poisoning is a silent, invisible killer. You just go to sleep before you can register a problem, and you never wake up again. Lisa had been killed by a chimney-full of snow.

We were inconsolable. Only a parent who has lost a child can possibly imagine what it feels like. If we hadn't had each other I don't know what would have happened.

For months we could barely function at all, as a song, or a word, would remind us that our daughter was never going to walk through the door again. We would never see her married, never hold her child, never hear her voice again. It was impossible to bear.

We discovered a group that was trying to bring awareness to the dangers of the insidious death that a blocked flue can bring. It seems so awfully tragic that young people, especially students living in rented rooms, should die this way so often, when a carbon monoxide detector can be bought for a few pence. We met one couple who had unbelievably lost *two* sons that way. A second son had been visiting his student brother at his digs when the gas fire in the sitting room malfunctioned, and both their children had died.

Over the last eleven years 437 people have needlessly lost their lives to carbon monoxide poisoning. Trying to stop further deaths was their legacy, the only one they could give the children who had unnaturally died before their parents. Surviving grief is different for everyone, but I feel that the way you cope with it can depend on your spirituality. If you have something to hang onto, some promise of feeling that child's hand again, or holding them, or hearing their sleepy voice whisper in your ear as you carry them up to bed, or even just a faith that they still exist somewhere, somehow, it can make all the difference. If you believe that somewhere they continue, then you have a chance, a hope of recovering.

Roger and I didn't really have any specific beliefs, but we were open-minded to the prospect of life carrying on after death. We just didn't know what we could do to nurture that possibility into a fact, so that it could help us get over this tragedy.

Then one day our other daughter, Lesley, said she thought we ought to go to a Spiritualist church, where there were mediums who claimed to be in contact with dead loved ones of the congregation.

We decided to give it a try, as we were ready to clutch at any hope. The first few visits were strange and not really convincing, and yet we felt they were helping us in some small way, so we carried on going. Then we met a young medium called Stephen Holbrook. Steve was amazing. He heard spirits rather than seeing them, in other words he was clairaudient, and we watched session after session as he brought incredibly convincing evidence to groups of people, proving to them that their loved ones were still around them. People would cry with joy at his meetings.

I am an incredibly sceptical person – Steve and Roger say my feet are stuck in concrete, but even I was convinced. Even though, try as he might, Steve didn't get a direct message from Lisa, from the evidence I saw, at least I knew that she must still exist on some level, like all the others that did come through.

My life was healed to a large degree.

Of course there were still times when the pain of loss were unbearable, like when Lisa's pupils invited us to the ballet school for a performance dedicated to her memory. I could barely see through my tears. But, on the whole, knowing she was somewhere, even if I couldn't see her or touch her, was some comfort. It brought me back from the brink.

We went to many other mediums' demonstrations, and came to realize quite soon that Steve was exceptional. The others brought us nothing but disappointment. So convinced were we of Steve's amazing gift that we decided to work with him, helping to promote him, and when we moved to Somerset we started organizing demonstrations for him there. We wanted to reach, and help, as many grieving souls as we could.

I used to ask Steve why he thought I wasn't getting a direct sign or message from Lisa, and he said that he often felt her there, next to him, but she never spoke. That was just like Lisa. She was always retiring, and never pushed herself forward. Even her incredible talent as a ballerina had to be coaxed out of her. Steve said that one day, when I was ready, Lisa would find a way to make something amazing happen to give me what I yearned for.

It was on my birthday, almost two years after Lisa's death, that we had snow again – just as we had when she died. Unusually for me, I felt compelled to walk the dog myself, rather than huddle in the warm kitchen by the Rayburn, hoping someone else would do it. I felt good in the crisp air as I stepped out with Rupert our Lurcher dog (a cross between a sighthound, such as a whippet, and a working breed, such as a collie) gamboling at my heels. The snow looked beautiful as I entered the woods, sparkling on the leaves and branches in the pale winter sun. It was crunchy underfoot, and I got childlike pleasure from leaving my tracks in the virgin white, as it was too early for anyone else to have been about.

When I came to the fork in the path, I thought about taking the shorter way home as I was looking forward to going out for my birthday lunch, but Rupert was still full of beans and made it obvious he wanted to continue the walk up into the fields. He dashed off, almost as if he was following someone, and I smiled at him and followed him uphill. I crossed the stile into the field, and Rupertpicked up a scent, as Lurchers do, and raced off along the hedgerow, while I carried on across the expanse of snow-covered grass.

As I reached the centre of the field, I stopped, stunned. In the snow at my feet, a name had been pressed into the snow. L I S A.

I looked around the letters in amazement because there was not a single footprint in the snow around it. Lisa had found a way.

One Moment in Time by Jill Prior (Apex Publishing, 2006)

How amazing that Jill and Roger's daughter found a way to use the very substance that killed her, snow, to bring them hope and comfort. Up until this point whenever they'd seen snow, their hearts had sunk as they were reminded of losing her, but after this experience, snow must have taken on a whole new, joyous meaning for them.

*

A Dad's Special Touch

Tess Smith

In 2002, my Dad passed away and I was totally beside myself

with grief. Carrying on without his guidance and protection seemed unthinkable. I was unable to sleep properly for weeks afterward. I wondered if I would ever sleep well again. Then one night, a miracle happened. I was lying in bed yet again not being able to get to sleep, when I felt Geoff, my husband, smoothing my hair. I was suddenly feeling quite calm and relaxed, as a feeling of peace crept over me – something I hadn't felt since Dad had died. It was Geoff; surely it had to be Geoff? But at the same time I could hear Geoff snoring.

I looked towards him and I realized it wasn't in fact my husband smoothing my hair. He was asleep, still, his hands in repose. You'd think I'd be scared that someone was touching my hair and I couldn't see them, but instead I was still really calm.

Loving the feeling, I tried my best to stay awake to keep it for as long as I could, but eventually I had to give in, and I fell asleep. It was the best night sleep I'd had in weeks.

I'll never know for sure who it was, who came to give me comfort as I have lots of family in spirit, but I will never forget that night...ever. I've had a few of these kinds of experiences but this one will always stay with me, as I was totally grief-stricken at the time, and it got me through.

Dads and daughters have a very special bond, and in this case Tess's Dad obviously knew when his little girl needed his gentle touch.

*

Becks Came Through For Her Dad

Irene Ellis

My daughter, Rebecca, was diagnosed with epilepsy in 1998. Although the diagnosis made us unhappy and uneasy, little did we guess that 18 months later she would actually be dead.

One dreadful day she was having a bath, getting ready for a job interview, when out of the blue she had a seizure. As soon as I realized what was happening, I tried to lift Becks from the bath, but although the Paramedics arrived very quickly in response to my call, it was too late. The seizure was fatal.

My other daughter, Melanie, and I, were comforted after a while by the fact that we both firmly believed in the afterlife, but my ex-husband, Willis, was a total non-believer. It would take him experiencing something personally for him to have any faith. But on September 4th 2003, he rang Melanie and me in a highly excited state. He told us that when he'd come home that day, he'd seen his answer phone light flashing. When he'd pressed the button to hear the message, there was Rebecca's voice, clearly saying, "Hi Dad." This was three years after Rebecca had died.

Willis could hardly believe his ears and insisted that I visit his home to listen for myself - which of course I was anxious to do. It was most definitely my girl's voice. There was no doubt at all. It was the most wonderful moment.

Needless to say, Willis changed immediately from someone skeptical, into someone who believes very much in the spiritual. I think that's why Rebecca chose to get through to him, rather than me or Melanie. She knew he was the one who needed convincing. I'm very proud of her for managing to communicate with him. None of us fear death anymore, because we know she's waiting for us.

When the message came I emailed a pen friend in Tyne & Wear to tell her about it, and discovered an amazing coincidence. She had recently been to a secondhand book sale and bought a copy of *Phone Calls from the Dead* (by researchers Rogo & Bayless). A tattered bookmark was already inside, and on that particular page was a statement made by another father who had received a phone message from his deceased daughter saying, "Hi Dad." My friend immediately sent the book to me, complete with bookmark, and it remains one of my most treasured possessions.

This is the reverse of the previous case. Becks knew that her Dad was the one who needed opening up spiritually, and that she was the best one to do it. It's wonderful to realize that even after they've died, our loved ones still want the best for us, they watch over us and care about how we're progressing spiritually.

*

There is No Death and There is No End

Gwen Byrne

I was born in a small flat in East Ham, the East End of London. I grew up nervous and highly strung as I was full of consuming questions about what happened to people when they died. Because of the lack of satisfactory answers, I developed a fear of churches and funerals, but I would walk for hours in cemeteries puzzling over where all the dead people had gone. I just knew they had to be somewhere.

In 1947 I went to London to work, and there I met a very good looking young man, called Arthur. My parents were able to put him up in their home and one thing led to another, ending with us getting married in 1950.

We had three sons, Kevin, Russell and Gary. From the day Russell was born I feared I would lose him. Even as a young child he needed a live-saving operation for a gangrenous appendix. All through his short life I saw signs that one day I would have to let him go. It tormented me. I remember one incident when Arthur and I were trying to buy all three boys new clothes. We got everything we wanted, except that none of the shops seemed to have Russell's size in anything. My heart sank, and the dreadful fear rose up in me again, that he wasn't going to live long enough to need them.

He was small for his age, but that didn't stop him from doing everything the other boys did. He won all his races at school, climbed trees, and tore around on a bike that was too big for him. To know him was to love him. He was adored by everyone.

In 1963 he was struck down with stomach pain, and I was certain the time I'd been dreading had come. I'd been very concerned over how thin he'd become. The doctors operated at once and found a huge malignant stomach tumor. They told me he had hours to live. He hung on a lot longer than that as it turned out, but within a short time he had gone. He was nine and three quarters.

All I could think of was his little face on the pillow; his beautiful navy-blue eyes closed for ever, his long lashes lying on his cheeks.

A Catholic priest tried to comfort me, saying, "Do not fear. Your son will go straight to heaven."

"How do you know this?" I demanded, "And how do you know there's a place called heaven?"

As always there was no satisfactory answer.

Nothing mattered anymore. The days dragged on and on. My mind constantly whirled with thoughts like, *Where is he? Will I ever see him again?* I started reading books to while away the dreary days, and I came across a book called *Spiritual Healing.* I wrote to the author to ask to be put on an absent healing list, ready to clutch at any straw. It seemed to help, and I did feel a little better. This encouraged me, and I read another book called, *Forty Years a Medium,* by Estelle Roberts. Then I started to read everything I could find about spiritualism, not mentioning it all to Arthur at first, because he still had his faith in his church.

I started to visit the local Spiritualist Church, where there were mediums, and I was pleased one day to come home from a meeting to find Arthur half-way through reading one of my books.

"I wonder how you get in touch with these people," he said.

I set out to try, and had some success. After a while one

medium drew a picture of Russell. It was incredible, and when I compared the drawing to a photograph of him, the likeness was 100% accurate. Although I still didn't know where Russell was, this gave me immense hope that he was reachable.

There followed many visits by me and .Arthur to various mediums, and we started to get constant little tidbits that proved to us that Russell was indeed trying to get through. All the messages we received though were spoken through the medium, and what I really longed for was to hear Russell's own voice.

As the proof that the messages were indeed from the spirit world grew, I started to wonder why everyone didn't know about this. Why didn't everyone who had lost somebody *know* that they still existed and that communication was possible? It's all so simple! The problem is that religion sees spiritual manifestations as supernatural, and they are not. There could be nothing more natural.

I needed to see Russell. My mother's heart cried out for one more glimpse. The first time I almost achieved this was due to my own developing skill at meditation. I saw a shape appearing in front of me and it gradually coalesced into Russell's hands. Then his sweater started to take shape, just as I had knitted it, the neckband, and his little neck. His chin appeared and his lips. I thought excitedly, *I'm going to see him!*

But by getting excited I must have spoilt the energy and stopped what he was trying to do, because he vanished. He tried to materialize again for me and that time I got his feet and legs and body, all the way up to his head, but again my emotions got the better of me and I spoilt it. Another time, although I didn't see anything, I felt Russell plant a tender kiss on my forehead, and then he leaned over me and I could actually feel his heartbeat. I knew then that what he was trying to do was show me that those in the spirit world can still have physical form.

Nineteen years to the day from when Russell had passed away, the moment I had been praying for finally came. Arthur received a phone call with the astounding news that Russell had introduced himself to a psychic circle in the Midlands, and incredibly that this was a direct voice phenomenon – in other words, Russell was speaking to the group himself and not through the voice of a medium. He told the group where we could be reached and that he wanted to talk to us! We immediately made plans to travel to a séance as soon as we could.

It's hard for me to convey my feelings as Arthur and I sat, holding hands at the séance.

When I heard those words, "Hello Mum, hello Dad! It's Russell! It's Russell!" I was so moved that I could scarcely speak, and I hardly remember the rest of that evening. I only know that my dear son chatted to us as if he had come back from popping out for a bag of sweets. The evening was full of laughter, with Russell seemingly taking charge of the whole thing. At one point he told us he had a gift for us and a pile of Liquorice Allsorts sweets tumbled onto our laps.

After that the days seemed unreal, and only the evenings, when I talked to my son, had any substance to them. My times with him seemed more concrete than any other. We had many conversations with Russell when he spoke of personal things that only he could know. Apart from the fact that the voice was definitely his, no-one else would have known the things he did. It wasn't just random messages either, I actually had full conversations with him and he answered questions easily with no hesitation, leaving me without a shred of doubt that I was talking to Russell himself.

When asked if he was still the boy he'd been nineteen years previously, and if time stood still in his world, he answered, "I can change all the time. I can be nine and three-quarters or I can be a big man, just like magic. Whoosh!"

At the Christmas séance a whole load of apports (materialized articles) appeared in the form of a pile of presents. When the candle was lit so that we could see them, pride of place went to a big pink panther toy. When we asked who it was for, there was the sound of small running feet coming towards us and the toy was laid across our laps. It was the most wonderful time.

All good things come to an end however, and it got to a point where we couldn't keep rushing up and down the country. Russell had achieved what he had set out to do.

He said he wanted me to know that there was no need for tears, and that everyone could talk to people who had passed over. He explained that the medium was just like a TV or radio, and necessary in order to 'download' the signal, so that we could hear and see it.

At one of the last séances we went to, Russell was charging round the room with an ordinary torch held in a red sock. He shone it on his feet, legs and hair, all of which I instantly recognized. Someone had suggested getting a pair of shoes to fit him and painting them with luminous paint. It was quite a sight to see those little glowing feet running around the room. He stood on his head on the sofa and put the shoes up against the wall so that we could all see them.

I wanted to know why we couldn't just put the light on, but it was explained that what we were dealing with was a chemical process, a bit like developing a photograph in a darkroom, and the light would destroy it. However, nowadays of course we have the ability to use infra-red lights and cameras, so soon we will be able to produce a film of an etheric body materializing. But it didn't matter that the light was out back then – it was very easy for me to know that Russell was in the room with me. What mother could doubt it?

Russell by Gwen Byrne [Janus, London, 1994, published in hardcover]

Some people can get by with just a sign, but Russell knew his Mum needed more from him. Having spoken to Gwen about her son I know he's a very progressive person, even in spirit, and has gone to great lengths to give her enough evidence to convince others of the existence of the spirit world.

*

They Still Care About Us

Alice Jean

When my mother was going through chemotherapy many years ago, my sister Barbara and I traveled from Texas to the north of USA and spent the month of November with her. Our plan was to return to see her again in the spring. Mom called me, I think in March, to say that she knew she wouldn't be there in the spring. She wanted Barbara and I to know, that she loved us, and that since Dad had already passed on, it didn't matter if we made her funeral or not. There were enough siblings and relatives up there for that. She knew our financial situation too wasn't really going to allow for another trip.

Mom passed away shortly after that phone call. Barbara and her husband were to come to our house a week later to visit, and we would all pray a rosary for Mom, and have our own little ceremony of remembrance for her.

People who have prayed the rosary will know what I'm talking about, when I say, I just kind of zone out while in this prayer.

We were at the table. Barbara and were I sitting side by side, facing the glass sliding doors to the patio. About one decade of beads (ten) had been prayed, when all of a sudden, there was Mom, just like that! She stood on the other side of the glass doors and gave a little wave of her hand.

She began to talk to me of the last letter and photo that I'd sent to her the previous week. The photo was to show her my new curly perm and ask how she liked it. Of course she'd had no chance to answer the letter, she said, because she died! I don't know why, but her appearance didn't startle me one bit, and I never skipped a beat with the prayers either. When we finished the rosary, we all got up and headed for the coffee pot. As soon as our husbands had gotten their coffee and moved away, Barbara whispered to me, "Did you see Mom?"

That startled me. Being the oldest sister and the one to take charge, I started asking questions like, "What was she wearing? What did she look like? Did she say anything?"

Here's the amazing part... Mom's talk to me about my hair and how happy she was was totally different from the conversation she had with Barbara!

Even though Mom had said she was OK about it if we couldn't go to her funeral, we'd still felt bad about it. But after her 'visit' it was all OK. I still talk to Mom after all these years, like she's right here.

Barbara's Perception of the Same Incident

One day while I was deep in prayer for my mother, with my eyes closed, I saw my father's face. He was wearing a very concerned look. He had passed on about four years previously.

I felt that he was telling me that he was also worried for my mother's soul.

About two weeks later I received a letter from my younger sister, back home, saying that mom had been to the doctor and that he felt that she had cancer. That made me really worried about her. I didn't feel that she was ready to go home. I prayed and prayed, but knew that if she passed away, there would be no way for me to know if she was OK or not until it was my time to go.

After my mom had been in treatment for a while, my older sister, Alice Jean, my two young daughters and myself, all made the trip home to be with mom.

Mom had lost all her hair due to the treatment, and she looked pale with sunken cheeks. When we returned home six weeks later, I still had my doubts as to whether or not mom was ready to go. But, she passed away four months after we returned home.

We were not able to make another trip. The day that she passed I asked God if He would give me some kind of sign to let me know that mom made it home.

A few nights later my family and I went to Alice Jean's house, and we all said the rosary for my mother. I had forgotten all about asking God for a sign. Shortly after we began to pray, I saw a lady appear, dressed in a white long dress. She was smiling and very happy. She had a full head of hair that was curly, and her cheeks were full and healthy looking.

She was floating, and she must have realized that I was trying to figure out who she was, because she said, "Look it's me, mom." She was my healthy mom, the one I used to know, with no lost hair.

She said, "Look what I can do!" as she floated upside down and sideways. She told me she made it home and was happy, and waved to me when she said good-bye.

After we finished praying I asked my sister if she had seen mom and she said she had. Then I remembered that I had asked God for a sign and I thanked Him for allowing me, the one that had been judging, to know that my mom had made it safe home.

Alice and Barbara's stories came to me from Texas. Spirits know no boundaries, and to them the world is a tiny place.

How amazing that these two sisters each saw and heard a different version of events, and yet they both obviously happened. Their Mum must have known just what to say and do to reach each of her girls.

*

An Old Soul in a Young Body

Margaret Prentice

When our son Richard was eight, he was diagnosed with Acute Lymphoblast Leukemia. It was a terrible shock and my husband Roy and I were living in a nightmare from that moment on. We both fought our emotions to keep this dreaded secret from Richard. At that time all I could think of was my pain and sorrow at what was going on in and around Richard. Nothing anyone said or did could comfort me. I was so absolutely enveloped in my own misery. The fear of knowing that my little boy might die in pain was almost unbearable.

He thought his Mum had everything under control as usual, and that nothing could harm him while she was around to protect him. What a great burden that is for a mother to carry. We know the doctors tried everything they could to save Richard, but he died – he actually died!

To try to make sense of it all I went on a search for some answers. Apparently Richard had the same idea in his world, because my broken heart was mended as Richard gradually made his presence known. He gave me proof of his continued existence in the most amazing ways. Every year on the anniversary of his death we got a sign from him at 4.20pm – the time he died. They varied from butterflies settling on me and refusing to leave, to gifts mysteriously appearing in my bed.

One time I was looking for a new blouse, and I found one that I knew Richard would like. I asked him for a sign that I was right, when suddenly all the alarms went off in the shop. There was only me and the assistant there, and she looked at me, shocked. She said, "Oh isn't that strange, it appears that we have a ghost in here, I hope you're not frightened."

I thought, *"Yes we have got a ghost in here, and I know who that ghost is!"*

Our other son Simon, was a drink and drug addict. During Richard's illness his behavior was another heavy load and an awful worry for us. I think he was worse because he loved his little brother so much, and yet, like us, he was powerless to help him.

Poor Simon died all alone one night in April 1994, aged 29. But he soon made us aware that he was still around too. Not long before he died he'd told me not to throw a pair of thick, heavy boots away. I got a message from him through a medium, "Mum, you can throw my boots away now. I won't need them here. I'm so sorry for all the aggro I caused you."

I'm still grieving after twelve years, and no doubt I will be grieving till the day I die. Grief is the same as love, it goes on and on. There is one difference though – Love is everlasting – even when we die we go on loving our loved ones, but grief ends with our death because we are reunited with our loved ones. And compared to life eternal in the spirit world, this life on earth is just a flash in the pan.

An addition to this is that my husband, Roy, totally believes too, now that he has had experiences far beyond mine. This is one he had years ago after I'd been trying EVP (Electronic Voice Phenomenon) - I did get a voice I believe is Richard's saying, "Mummy".

This is what I wrote to a friend in 1994.

'This was not the end... spirit pestered Roy for years and occasionally they still come to him but are much more gentle now they know he understands. I was away in Scotland with my niece last week, leaving my husband Roy to look after our aged cat. Roy told me when I got home that he had had a visitation *again* from someone who he thinks is our son Simon, who died in 1994 from a overdose of pain killers and sleeping tablets.

This has apparently been going on for about 3 years, sometimes twice a week and sometimes only once a month, but it has got regular lately. He hears someone come in through his bedroom doorway and come round to his face and breathes in his face and gets his wrists and pins him to the bed, and gets him round the neck in a head lock, as in wrestling. Once a voice said in a whisper, "Roy..Roy... Simon, I'm going to kiss you," then he felt a big kiss planted on his forehead.

When this arm is round his neck, it's so strong that Roy can't get it away, even trying to prize it off, but then it releases him and he hears laughter. Roy swears at it and when it's coming round the bed he shouts at it, "Simon, is that you...you B......?" Then it sits on the bed next to him and Roy sees the bed go down, and feels a big body weight there. He said the arm is solid flesh and the body weight like a full grown man.

When I asked Roy who he thinks it is, he said, "Oh it's Simon all right. I know it is."

Well it might be that, since I have been asking spirit to put a voice on my recorder. I asked them to go to Dad if they can't get me. I said let him know you're real and make him understand that it's not rubbish. (I only got what I asked for!) Roy is not afraid of it... just annoyed because it even wakes him up pushing him out of bed. I suspect that after I asked them to make Roy know they are around - it being in the night when I asked - I bet they went straight to him. (That was about 3 years ago).

He told my medium friend last week, the day after it happened the last time. She prayed and asked them to leave him alone now that he knows, and afterwards he told me everything is quiet again.

Don't it make you think? Be careful what you ask for. You probably will get it. I have found that to be true so many times. Nothing as real as this though.

Roy is a good man and sensible, so if he says anything it is definitely true. He's always said he knows something is there, but he don't want to get involved in it all.

Lucky spirit went to him, because I think if that had happened to me I'd be afraid. Even knowing it is my loved ones.

This is wonderful evidence for me.

My son Richard used to jump on us in bed on a Sunday morning and wrestle Roy and get him round the neck like that and shout "MIT... MIT..." (submit) - and Roy would either say, "Yes, yes," or I'd have to help hold his shoulders down for a fall.

Weird stuff isn't it? They did come back for a while, when I asked them if they were still around... But now they've been quiet for a few weeks.

I hope it stays that way, even though I know it is our loved ones. It was really getting Roy down. He used to lay and wait for it to happen. Always around 12.30am to 1.30am. Now that they have let me know they still exist, we think they're happy that they got through to me, through Roy.'

Margaret Prentice is author of a book *Richard, Spirit and I*

Richard and his brother kept their mischievous natures, even in spirit, and mundane sounding messages, such as the one about the boots, are far better proof that the person really is hearing from their loved ones than anything else. This is because the chances of a fake medium knowing these small personal facts, is so remote as to be non-existent.

*

A Special Christmas Gift

Debbie Branscombe

I was not particularly close to my Mum as a child. I'm the eldest of three. When we were young I was my father's favourite, and we were very, very close. We went to live in New Zealand in 1987, and whilst we were there my father left my mum, after thirty years of marriage.

With my Dad out of the picture, my relationship with my

Mum blossomed. We became extremely close; inseparable. She was like my other half, my best friend, and we seemed to have a very spiritual link. She was told by a medium that she had the gift, but it frightened her a little and she never pursued it, but she never doubted the spiritual side of things.

My first paranormal experience happened when I was about five years old. My Nan died, and a couple of days later she came to see me and asked me to give my Mum a message. She was wearing very bright white, which seemed to shine and shimmer. She took hold of my hand and then suddenly I was in a beautiful garden. It had steps leading into the garden and at the far end was a gate that led out over a bridge into the countryside. The flowers were so bright, yellows and blues and so beautiful. There were tables in the garden covered in white table cloths and there were other beings there, but I couldn't quite make out any other faces. I just know that they all felt very loving and friendly and seemed to be smiling. It was a bit like a garden party or a village fete! My Nan told me to tell my Mum that she was fine. I remember, I wanted to go through the gate at the end of the garden to the bridge, but she told me I could not go out that way and that I had to go back down the steps the way I came.

Anyway I gave my Mum the message which she accepted straight away.

About twenty years later, tragically, my Mum got cancer. After suffering all sorts of different treatments, she became quite ill and I looked after her. We made a promise to each other that whoever passed over first would come back and let the other one know that they were OK, even if it meant that we might scare each other.

I promised my mum that I would be with her at the end, and I stayed up with her all night as she fought so hard, but I just popped downstairs to get a cup of tea, and although I was only gone two minutes, when I came back, Mum had gone. I wasn't with her when she died, like I'd promised her, and I felt I had let her down.

For the first six weeks afterwards I spent every spare moment at the cemetery, and could not be consoled. My grief was all consuming, and so was my guilt at not having kept my promise to be with her when she died. Somehow, you feel that you can't go on without the one you have become so a part of, it is almost like losing half your soul.

What was even worse was that she didn't keep her promise to come back and let me know that she was OK. After a while I lost all my beliefs, and any hope of life after death. I decided that when we die, we just die, and that's it. And I thought that if that was the case, then what was the point of it all?

About five months later, my best friend, Pat, who lives about two hundred miles away, telephoned me and asked if she could come and stay for Christmas. She was very insistent, and said that she needed to come. She was not at all well herself, and wanted me to give her some support. I didn't really want to celebrate Christmas, I didn't feel like any company and I certainly didn't feel strong enough to give anyone else my support, but her daughter convinced me to let them come.

The evening they arrived things were a bit odd. Pat didn't feel too good, and Debbie (her 18 year old daughter) was very uneasy. I kept bursting into tears at the drop of a hat. Christmas without Mum was a bleak and cold prospect.

That night I talked and talked with Pat (and cried), and she told me my Mum had asked them to come to me. She had told Pat to tell me, "Thank you for the rose". (A gold rose brooch that I had placed in Mum's coffin and that no one else had known about). I didn't believe it – as far as I was concerned my Mum was gone forever.

Things were fairly tense for the next couple of days, because Pat kept insisting my mum was there, and I insisted just as strongly that she wasn't.

On Christmas Eve, Pat called me upstairs, to where her daughter was sitting on my bed crying, saying that she couldn't cope with it any more. I asked her what she was talking about and she told me that my Mum's presence was almost suffocating her.

I said that if my Mum *was* there it would be for me and that I would know about it. I put my arm around Debbie to comfort her. When I did, it was like being hit by an electric current; it nearly knocked me over, and I knew that it was my Mum.

That night I stayed downstairs, hugging myself with the dawning knowledge that there *was* something after death, and that my Mum was keeping her promise.

I could feel this vibration coming all over me. It made me jump, but in the end I said, "okay, come on Mum. I can deal with this, and I won't panic."

I lay down on the floor and closed my eyes and tried to be open and relaxed for whatever was to come. I clearly felt someone put two cushions on the floor behind me and lay down. Then I felt wonderful warmth as she put her arms around me and cuddled me. I leaned back, and could feel all of her. I was trying to be rational, and I pinched myself, but she was really there supporting my weight. We had quite a chat and I asked lots of questions. I asked her why it had taken so long for her to come through, as she'd promised, and she said she had, but I had never Shut UP! Because of that I hadn't heard her.

She said when she first crossed over she didn't know what to do and was sort of in a large waiting building with a queue all around the building. (No rest from queues then – even after you die!). But she was fine now. She had a job to do over there helping others who had crossed over with cancer.

She told me she had seen her Mum (my Nan), and her Dad and sister. She and her sister had been visiting me and watching over me during my grief, holding my hand and stuff. They had even tried to pull the bedclothes off to get my attention, but I was too wrapped up in myself to see or hear anything.

I had the best Christmas ever after that. The depression was gone, it was just incredible. I've seen Mum a couple of more times since then, and she plays the odd joke on me, just to make me jump I think.

I am a Reiki healer, but since this experience I also do spiritual healing by asking the spirits for help and letting them work through me. It is absolutely fantastic when they come through. Not only do I feel them but so does the person I am touching.

The spirit world went to so much trouble to get through to me. It took two people who lived two hundred miles from me, and six months. Spirit did not just talk to me, I felt them, I was actually held, and my weight was supported. It was truly the most wonderful thing that has ever happened to me and I will never forget it.

When Mum came back it changed me. I no longer have any fear of death, maybe of pain, but not death. Of course I would never wish to leave my family, but I know that I will see my Mum again one day. In turn, I have also promised my sons, believers or non-believers, that I will let them know that I'm OK when I pass, even if I have to kick them up the bum!

I don't hear from her that often anymore although I often feel she is around. However, my first granddaughter was born just two weeks ago and she was certainly about then, she was so excited. Before the baby was born, in the early stages, I asked the spirits whether it was a boy or a girl, I could not get anything through so I kept asking is it blue for a boy or pink for a girl. I thought I might at least get a color – nothing came through. That night I dreamt and everything was pink, pink grass, pink trees, pink sky. Anyway I woke up immediately and said thanks I get the picture and told everyone the next day. No one believed me and everyone thought it would be a boy, I even doubted myself... silly me, pink trees pink grass. Of course my little girl is now two weeks old, and she has been named Elanor Miriam. Miriam was my mother's name.

It seems that some of us resist seeing or hearing messages from beyond, because we're frightened to hope. Debbie had resigned herself to her loss, and was afraid to upset her equilibrium by feeling what was coming through. Her Mum was very determined to make sure her daughter finally got the message, and once she did, the door was open.

Chapter Two

Signs, Portents, Warnings and Rescues from Spirit

It seems that even once they've passed over, our friends and loved ones continue to worry about us, just as we continue to worry about them. So much so, that when they see that we're about to make a big mistake, or when something is coming to us that they know we might have trouble coping with, they feel the need to make great efforts to send us a message or warning. Just as on Earth a father, mother or much loved brother, sister or close friend would literally do anything to help us, so this caring never ends, even after death.

*

Dad Saved Me

David Bryant

I was alone, and it was late, perhaps just after midnight. I was in the area around RAF Coltishall, where I had sprinkled my Dad's ashes in the River Bure just a few weeks earlier. Dad had been a Flight Sergeant in the RAF.

Rounding a bend near the airbase, I was forced to halt at a red light at the beginning of a long stretch of roadworks. These had restricted the carriageway to just a single track for two hundred meters. It was a very isolated spot and as far as I could see mine was the only car around. I drummed my fingers on the steering wheel impatiently, before resigning myself to spending an apparently unnecessary few minutes' wait for non-existent on-coming traffic. I mused that it was about time that all traffic lights on such quiet stretches of road were able to tell when there were no vehicles coming, and let you through automatically.

I rested my eyes while I waited. Suddenly I felt the familiar touch of my recently deceased father on my shoulder. There was no doubt of the identification: I recognized the firm yet light caress too well to be mistaken. It was my Dad. His hand gripped my shoulder and my eyes flew open as a tinge of warning fizzed through my mind. I had to get my car out of there!

There was no doubt about what I was being bidden to do. I threw my vehicle into reverse and accelerated backwards away from the traffic light. At that very instant a black Ford Capri, running only on side lights, hurtled around the bend at the other end of the roadworks, and, apparently not under control, careered through the very spot where my car had been until seconds before. The car skidded and snarled past me and then rapidly disappeared into the distance.

I blew out a relieved breath, and then, was it my imagination, or did I hear the low, throaty chuckle, which I had resigned myself never to hear again in this world?

It was a good job David was already someone attuned to spirits, otherwise this might have ended badly.

*

Love Binds Us Together

Jane Davidson

I was just thirteen years old. A couple of weeks earlier my little eight year old sister had been knocked down by a car and had died. How can a child the age I was try and understand or even cope with a sudden bereavement like that. One minute she was there, large as life, and apparently immortal, and then like a candle flame snuffed out, she was gone. I couldn't grasp it at all.

I lay alone in my bed, devastated and shell-shocked, just wanting my sister back with all my heart.

I used to share that room with my sister, but now it was empty and cold. I lay facing the wall, turning my back on the world that had suddenly become so harsh, trying to sleep and trying to make sense of what had happened, when suddenly I had a very strong sense of someone else in the room. I knew someone was standing behind me at the side of the bed, but I also knew that no other member of the family had come into the room, because if they had, the light on the stairs would have flooded the room when they opened the door.

I was too terrified to call out to anyone. I lay there bathed in sweat until eventually I got the courage to turn over and see who was there. It was my sister. She looked as solid and she ever had in life and she was dressed in clothes I had never seen before. (I later found out these were the clothes she had been buried in). My sister spoke to me saying, "Please don't cry anymore. I am fine and we will be together again one day, and when that day comes it will seem like a moment that we have been apart."

This connection with the spirit world changed my whole perception of what we really are. I was truly blessed that day and the comfort it brought to me was indescribable. The sadness didn't go away, because even though I knew my sister still existed, she wasn't going to be there for me in a physical sense any more, and I would miss that forever. The grieving process doesn't go away despite the blessing of a visitation by someone you have lost, however knowing that they are somewhere else and still 'alive' in some way was a huge comfort to me and still is. So, you can see why I absolutely believe in the spirit world and my angels. I have been given the evidence that these powers truly exist.

By opening the mind and heart anyone can see and experience these wonderful things for themselves. I believe that everyone has some level of psychic ability. However, not every psychic can be a medium but every medium is a psychic, in my opinion.

It's like learning a musical instrument. Most people can learn to play the piano if they put their mind to it, some practice hard to become a good player and a few have a natural talent that enables them to add interpretation, feeling, write songs or become a concert pianist. This analogy applies to every walk of life (sport, art, business) and we are guided individually towards our own natural talents. Who knows, maybe it is the spirits and angels who really guide us. Whether we choose to listen or not is another matter.

To me, love never dies. Love is the link that binds us all together, whether in the physical body or as spirit. It is everlasting love that drives us and spirits to communicate and bridge the gap between the physical and spirit worlds. A medium is merely a means to bridge that gap and facilitate the communication.

Sometimes we all get very powerful dreams that transcend earthly troubles and take us to a connection of souls, which is actually so much more real than worldly arguments. I was lucky enough to have such a dream, which changed the course of my troubled relationship with my mother.

I dreamt one night that my Mum was going to die. It was a very powerful dream and although I didn't feel frightened when I awoke I felt quite disturbed by it. It played on my mind all day and that evening I rang my elder sister to discuss it with her. Mum and I had fallen out, and I was very worried that she would actually die, not knowing I loved her and not knowing whether she loved me either. I decided it was worth the risk in trying to talk to her (not about the dream but our relationship).

I did make the call and how glad and blessed I was. Against all odds Mum understood what I was saying and we really talked for the first time in our lives. From that one phone call we rang each other almost every day and were making all kinds of plans to go out and do the things I had always wanted to do with her. Sadly that element of the story never came to anything as Mum was found dead at home about a month after my dream. I see this as a blessed gift from spirit to give our family the opportunity to make amends and find each other even for such a short time. The evening before Mum died she rang me at about 8.30pm and the last words she ever spoke to me were, "I love you Jane." I won't ever forget those words.

My third experience was with my sister, Susie. When she was just 32, she died of breast cancer. Susie was always like a Mum to me, and yet at the same time she was always making us all laugh. Two years before she died, while she was already diagnosed as terminally ill, a medium, who didn't know about Susie, told me that she would be dead in two years time and would spend her birthday in heaven. She also said that Susie would have trouble leaving us and that I would be the one to tell her it was OK to go. I gave up my job to care for Susie.

Two years later, eight days before her birthday, Susie asked for me. She said, "I have to get better Janey!" She really wanted to stay with us, even suffering as she was. But there was no chance of it.

She asked me for Reiki healing, but what happened was some sort of soul to soul union. The sounds of the hospice faded around us and gradually the sound of footsteps started echoing around the room, until it seemed the area was filled with a crowd of people. I knew it was the rest of our family who were already in spirit coming to take Susie. I spoke to her on a soul level and said, "You've suffered enough. You should let go now."

And 30 seconds later, Susie was gone.

http://www.ki-lin.co.uk/

This must have been an incredibly difficult message to accept, being told that someone you loved was going to die, but I think this message about Susie came from their Mum. She knew how hard it would be for Jane to lose her sister, so she wanted to prepare her.

*

Don't Ignore Spirit's Advice

Russell Reynolds

On October 15th, three years ago, I and two friends drove to Boise, Idaho so that I could have open heart surgery. I needed to have four bypasses done as my arteries were 90% plugged. When we arrived in Boise, we had to find a motel room to stay in over night, as I had to be at the hospital at 6am the next morning. My Mom and brother were also going to be there, but they would be getting there a couple of hours later on.

We found a motel and checked in. We went to the room and took in our things for the night. We were sitting in the room for about 20 minutes when the phone rang and my care provider answered it. She got a funny look on her face and she said the phone was for me. No one knew where we were staying as I had not contacted anyone to let them know. I took the phone and a Spanish sounding voice on the other end asked if this was me.

I said, "Yes," and he said, "Don't have your surgery tomorrow. It's not your turn to die..."

I was floored; because no one who knew I was to have my surgery had been contacted. I asked "Who is this?" and he said, "It's Oscar."

The only person I knew by that named had died the year before of cancer. I had worked with him at the factory and he would stop every shift and talk to me. In the background I could hear hundreds of voices and I asked him where he was at and he said, "I am in between Heaven and Earth..."

Then he told me again not to have my surgery, as it was not my turn to die, and then the connection went dead. I could hardly believe that this had happened, and I told my friends about the phone call. I called my brother and told him about the call, but he and Mom were still about an hour away from Boise. He knew this friend, Oscar, as he worked at the same factory as we did. He told me that I'd better take the call seriously and they would see us in a little while and we would go and eat.

We discussed the phone call over dinner and my mother and brother both agreed that I had better talk to my doctor about it, at least about my concerns. The next morning we went to the hospital just before 6am and they started getting me ready. I asked to see my doctor and they told me he would be there in a few minutes. I looked through the door a few minutes later and he was pacing back and forth in tight circles in front of my door.

Then he came in and before I could tell him what had happened, he said that my surgery had been postponed for a week, and that the head doctor of the department would be in to see me in a few minutes. When the other doctor came in, he told me that the doctor who was scheduled to do the surgery had lost the last three patients he'd operated on, and they were all from my area. The head doctor had rescheduled my surgery for one week later and he would be doing the surgery himself.

One week later, I had the surgery and went through it without any problems.

I thank God that He allows our friends to warn us when it's not our turn to die. I also thank God for giving me a second chance and for giving us friends who care enough to change the future.

That wasn't the only time I got a message from spirit that I'm glad I listened to.

In January 2003, on the tenth of the month, my girlfriend, whom I was going to marry, passed away from lung cancer. Before she died, she told me that if she could contact me after she'd passed, she would do. A little over a month later I came back to my apartment about 11:30 pm. As the latch on the door clicked, I heard her voice say, "If you go to Jackpot tonight you'll win big..."

The hair on the back of my neck stood up and I got goose bumps all over. We used to go to Jackpot, Nevada, from time to time, and ten months before she had won almost $7,000.00 on a nickel slot machine.

I'd promised her that I would buy her a head stone, as her family could not afford to get her one. Well to make this a little shorter, I got in my car and drove the 90 miles to Jackpot and got down there at 1am. At 4:30am I hit a jackpot for $3,743.00 and over the next hour I hit two more jackpots for $1,000.00 each. I came home with over $5,000.00, and the first thing I did with the money was to buy my girlfriend's headstone, and I helped her kids by putting an inscription on the back of it.

She may be gone from this Earth but her spirit is still with me, and I feel her presence all the time. She will always be with me even if I should find someone else to love.

In this story from the USA, what a good friend Oscar turned out to be. How strange for him to call sounding as if he was on Heaven's subway! The second message just goes to show you, love survives everything. Russell's girlfriend is still looking out for him years after she passed away.

*

A Second from Death

Simon Ellis

I live in Spain nowadays, but if it wasn't for the help of a spirit, I wouldn't be living anywhere right now. It was just another day, a Sunday, with no signs that anything unusual was going to happen. It was sunny, as it almost always is here, and I felt relaxed and happy as I strolled down to the flea market. I was passing through the rough quarter as it was a great shortcut from my high-rise apartment on the outskirts to the shopping area. I loved the flea market, because there was hardly anything that wasn't for sale there, from mundane, every day items, to the unusual and sometimes outright bizarre. I was in a narrow street, and nothing was on my mind except warm anticipation of what I might find today.

Places like flea markets were vital to me, because I was gradually building a business as an interior designer. I specialized in helping ex-pats give their Spanish homes an authentic yet comfortable feel. They loved the very different items I found for them.

I was meeting my partner, Cerys, at the market, and I started seeing her in my mind's eye as a got closer to the city center. Suddenly I was snapped out of my daydreams by a voice. It wasn't a shout, just a quite authoritative voice right behind me, saying, "Simon!" I glanced back over my shoulder, without breaking stride, but there was no-one there.

It was a woman's voice and my first thought had been that Cerys had come to meet me and snuck up behind me, but it wasn't her, it wasn't anyone. I walked on. The voice came again, so clearly that I couldn't ignore it, "Simon! Stop! Right now!"

The voice had the same tone that my Mum's used to have when I was a kid, and she *really* meant 'right now'. I didn't have a choice. I stopped, rooted to the spot, and that's when it happened. I was three feet from a phone booth, and suddenly it was totally annihilated as part of a roof balustrade came crashing down on top of it. The block must have weighed half a ton, and if I'd been any closer I would have been killed. Parts of concrete shrapnel flew from the wreckage, smashing the window of the house behind the phone booth. I got some minor scratches to my arms and face, from the glass of the booth, and I was covered in dust, but apart from that I stood untouched by the virtual explosion that had happened feet from me. If I hadn't stopped I would have been right next to the phone booth that was now just a crumpled, crushed mess.

I'll never really know who called me. When I got to the market, Cerys was horrified at the state of me, but she was adamant it wasn't her who'd called out the warning. This experience changed my life somewhat as I really do feel that it means it isn't my time yet, that I have some specified role to play in the world that meant I wasn't allowed to die that day.

Was it an angel? My guardian angel maybe? Was it the voice of my Mum, who had died seven years before, using her maternal influence over me to make me listen? I have no idea, but I do know that I was saved by just about a second.

Of course a mother's love is legendary. Like a tigress defending her cubs, Russell's mum stepped in when her child was in danger. We'll all always be our mother's babies, even when we're on our own death beds, and I find that a very comforting thought.

Chapter Three

Reassurances

Often we find ourselves in a position of fear or nervousness in this frenetic world we live in. We seem to always have to push our boundaries and step outside our comfort zone. When we're pushed to the limit, this fear or distress seems to send a message out into the Universe, and sometimes if we're lucky, we get a response that amazes us.

The Tetchy Angel

Jenny Bishop

I've always been terrified of flying and I always swore that I'd never set foot on a plane. I was convinced that the plane would crash *just* because *I* was on it. But then I got the chance of a holiday in the one place that could tempt me; America. I'd always wanted to go there, but never dreamed that I would. I don't think my family would have forgiven me if I'd chickened out.

So I went. Things were not too bad, and I was coping better than I thought I would until we had a two hour delay in Detroit due to storms in the area. The last thing I wanted was to fly in a storm. But we finally boarded anyway and sat on the runway with the plane quivering in the wind, waiting for takeoff. The pilot didn't make me feel any better by announcing "...there are some real heavy storms coming in, but if the next inbound makes it, we'll give it a go." *Give it a go?* Was he mad?

Twenty minutes later I was in the grip of the nightmare I'd always feared. We'd taken off, and the crew was strapped in, lightning rent the air outside, the plane was being tossed around by a giant hand, and I was almost hysterical with terror. As the plane plunged around the sky like a mad mustang, even the crew started to look really scared. They couldn't leave their seats or they too would have been thrown around like rag dolls.

The plane was going to go down, just like I had always dreamed it would. I felt a scream rising in my throat.

Just then a blue haze appeared right in front of me. Before my very eyes stood a beautiful blue angel, with white feathered wings. The scream died in my throat. The angel leaned towards me, wrapping his wings around me. I looked to see if anyone else was amazed by this apparition, but it was obvious I was the only one who could see it. The angel spoke to me and he said, "Do not be afraid. I am holding the plane." Then he vanished. No pill or potion or hypnotic trance could have performed the transformation in me. I became totally calm.

But after a while logic kicked in and my euphoria wore off, as the plane showed no signs of stopping its aerial rodeo. I started to panic again. Back came the angel. He said the same thing and vanished. This happened a third time, and by then I think he was getting annoyed with me. He leaned in again and said quite forcefully, "You will *not* fall. *I* am holding the plane."

Unspoken were his un-angelic thoughts, *so for goodness sake let me get on with it and stop wasting my time!* I guess even angels can get tetchy.

Needless to say, we landed safely, and I have never been scared of flying since then.

Is it possible for an angel to physically hold up a plane? It seems to me that a fear this strong couldn't be controlled by anything except a real experience. Next time I fly I'll certainly be asking for some of this kind of protection!

*

He Came To Meet Her

Bobbette Wilkerson

Just a little background before I get to the story at hand. My grandfather (Papa) died on August 19, 1999. He had been on dialysis for four years and died in the hospital of heart failure. On Tuesday August 17th, he had told the doctor that he didn't have but two more days to live, and he was right.

We thought that we would lose my grandmother (Granny) not long after my Papa died, but she proved all of us wrong. She had taken care of him since the day he got sick and that was all she had known for four years. They had been married for over 56 years.

Fast forward to 2006. Granny was diagnosed with lung, bone, and stomach cancer on August 15, 2006. The following Wednesday she had a portal catheter put in to start chemo and on that Friday, the doctors found out she had 4th stage brain cancer. After finding out that she had the brain cancer she opted not to do chemo or have radiation and just to live out the rest of her days however God chose fit.

My parents had lived with my grandparents since my Papa had gotten sick and my kids and I only lived about seven miles from them. We were down there a lot, and after she was diagnosed with cancer, we were down there every day.

Two weeks before my Granny died we were down visiting, and she and I were sitting on the front porch. She looked at me and said, "Guess who came to visit me today?"

I was trying to guess who had stopped by to see her that maybe hadn't been around for a while. After a few wrong guesses, I finally said I didn't know who. Her reply was, "Papa."

Believing that this was very well possible, I asked her what had happened. She began to tell me how she had gotten up out of bed that morning, she went into the kitchen to fix herself some

41

toast to take with her medicine, and went back to her bedroom to watch TV. She had just sat down on the bed when he appeared at the window and started to walk over to her. Of course this caught her by surprise, and she started to cry. He simply told her that he was coming to get her soon. She asked him when and all he said was soon, then he just disappeared. She told me that she sat there for about an hour crying and asking him to come back just one more time.

On Friday, October 13th, we had gone down there to visit and she was a little slow but was still coherent. Just as my kids and I were about to leave, she asked me to wait for just 30 minutes. I told her that I couldn't and that we would be back down there first thing the next morning. By the time we arrived on Saturday, she was not coherent and could only keep her eyes open for about 30 seconds at a time the most. She died at 10:24 on Sunday, October 15th.

My mother said that before she took her last breath she smiled and waved. One of her sisters, who was there said, "Did you see her wave at us?"

My mother's reply was, "She wasn't waving at us, she was waving at the ones we couldn't see, the ones who came to get her."

I know that Papa was one of the ones who came to meet her, because he'd told her that he was coming to get her.

The one thing that I will regret until the day that I die is that I didn't wait just 30 more minutes the day before she died. If I had known what was about to happen, I would have stayed. I have learned the hard way not to take the people in your life for granted and cherish every single moment with them. You are never promised tomorrow, only the day at hand...

This truly beautiful story of a love that didn't die demonstrates the total joy in unconditional love. Love of this sort knows no boundaries. To 'Papa' his wife was as gorgeous and as loved as she was on the day he married her.

*

A Spirit's Influence

Josephine Sellers

As a family we were in a desperate plight. The 400 year old cottage that we had loved and lived in and brought up our family in for sixteen years, was being overwhelmed by a building development. Because the cottage sat on ancient land riddled in springs, the new building works nearby had upset the water table and flooded the land our cottage stood on. A moat had been dug around us by the developers, and we were left on an island surrounded by dirty water and the dreadful noise and upheaval of the building site. The cottage was beautiful, and we had opened the garden for years to raise funds for charity, but now it was hellish. The water problems obviously left us in a precarious position, and we had written to the planners about the problems but they could not or would not do anything to help.

The mental and physical strain was starting to take its toll. Words cannot describe the pain endured or the mental battles within. We felt alone and abandoned.

One evening, feeling desperate, I wrote a letter to the directors of the development company. The letter came from the heart and I begged them to review our position from a humanitarian point of view. They were in a position to give us our freedom by buying the cottage from us, and I appealed to them to do so, but they refused to negotiate, and I felt emotionally broken.

Unknown to me, at that time, my mother Gwendoline had consulted with a medium at a Spiritualist church, for her own personal reasons. At that meeting she was given a message for me from my dead father Joseph. My mother was not aware of our precarious situation, or my emotionally low state, and so she did not understand the message my father had given her for me, but she related it faithfully. He told her that all was not yet lost. He said that I was to telephone one particular director of the development company, and ask him to encourage his fellow directors to consider negotiating with us. My father assured me the result would be positive. It worked! Following weeks of delicate and painful negotiation, we finally settled on a sale figure. At last we could afford to move, and escape the conditions that had made our house no longer a home.

In the process I had received graphic evidence of how those that care for us, in other realities, can help us, if we are open to the possibility.

My Dad was 76 when he died of cancer, in a hospice. I'd sat by his bedside. It was summer time, I was looking out of the window at the view and a voice in my head said, 'he is going to take his last breath'. I looked at him and standing behind his bed were two women. He breathed in and never breathed out. He slipped away peacefully. Later when I described the two women to my mother – she said it was my father's mother, and one of his sisters.

The Return of Yesterday's People by Josephine Sellers (published by Capall Bann, 2002)

Josephine's father crossed the divide with vital knowledge that only a spirit could know, proving once again the amazing bond between father and daughter.

*

A Little Help From Nan

Jacqui Moran

Saturday night was a Psychic Supper night, you know the sort of thing, fish and chips supper with a ten minute reading from a medium. I had a really nice reading from the medium on our table and it was longer than ten minutes as she had so much to say. From what she said I realized that it was my Nan she had with her. Amongst other things, Nan said that she was helping to repair my broken heart, bless her. Pauline, the medium, said that Nan wanted me to remember Scarborough. Now I went there when I was about nine years old with Nan and my Aunt Jenny (who was Nan's sister). It was only for the day and a very nice day it was, but I couldn't remember too much about it now. Pauline said all Nan wanted to say about Scarborough was for me to remember it. Odd, I thought, as to why Nan would want me to remember that trip as we had many others that I could remember better!

Anyway, I'd not been feeling too well with one thing and another over the previous month and after I'd taken some time off sick my boss suggested I look for a holiday to have a rest as she knew I was getting to breaking point.

Sunday morning I thought some time away might be a good idea so I had a look on the internet for somewhere to go and I found a place that looked very nice but the main thing that attracted me was that they also offered holistic treatments like Reiki, detox and energy therapy. I desperately needed the energy therapy so that sounded like just what I needed right then. When I looked at the contact details I realized that this place, Fountain's Court, was in, of all places, Scarborough. I hadn't noticed that before.

Maybe Nan knew before I did that I'd go to this place and I wonder if she was pointing me in the right direction. When I spoke to the owner to see if she had vacancies, I explained what had happened on Saturday night and she told me that one of her early visitors (she had only been open a year) said that she was not to worry as guests would come and they would be guided to her holistic hotel. You know something, I think that person was right as my Nan certainly guided me, it seems.

Thanks Nan for sending me back to Scarborough for some much needed recuperation. I was really looking forward to my holistic break away, not doubting that my family would all be with me too, especially Nan.

So I had a fantastic week away, the hotel was really lovely, it had a very spiritual feel about it that you could pick up immediately you walked in. Had quite a few treatments, including the energy treatment (really needed that one), Emotional Freedom Technique (got rid of a lot of stuff there, I can tell you), foot massage, Indian head massage, and even a Japanese face lifting massage. I had an infra-red sauna every morning as well, and enjoyed that very much. I felt much pampered; especially as I was their only guest so I was very well looked after. I got plenty of fresh air with long walks along the sea front every day plus lots of walks around the beautiful park nearby.

My back problem is a whole lot better, in fact it doesn't hurt at all apart from the odd twinge now and again, so it was worth it just for that alone.

I can't thank my dear Nan enough for guiding me to this much needed holistic break; she obviously knew I needed it. I don't believe that this was just a coincidence either; it was planned by my family in spirit. Bless 'em.

http://www.fountainscourt.com

Chapter Four

Spirit Saviors

We sometimes find ourselves perched on the edge of a metaphorical, or sometimes a very real, abyss. In this position it's often hard to see any way back to safe ground. But there are miraculous escapes all the time.

Picture the child recovered from a flattened building, days after an earthquake. Why should she survive when everyone else has died?

Self-destruction and despair fed hopelessness can lead you very close to making a big mistake. Or you might find yourself on the verge of dying, and even accept it, only to have a spirit save you in a real and sometimes very physical way.

Spirits can intervene, and they do. If it's not your time to go, then it's just not.

Back From the Edge

Susie Anthony

I was dying. All my systems were shutting down as the cocaine hit harder and harder. My apartment in Johannesburg started to fade around me, and I was glad. I was eager to leave the world and this seemed like a relatively easy way to go.

Then suddenly I felt as if I was snatched up and I opened my eyes in shock. I was in the air, floating above my body which lay beneath me on the floor, twitching in its last death throes. It wasn't a pretty sight, and I saw my life as it had really been.

As a child, I'd dreamed of being special, of making a difference. I'd dreamed of being a doctor and helping people. I'd seen myself caring for people and making them well. However, the challenges of my young years had driven these dreams into the realms of pure fantasy.

My mother was from a poor and humble background. She was lucky to even have a pair of shoes to wear. My father was a drinker, a gambler and a few things worse than that so we never had much money in our home either. Many times Dad squandered all the money and we didn't even have food to eat. When he left, my mother and I had no home and no money. This situation was so hard on me that I determined that I would never be poor again. In my fear and desperation to survive, I forgot about helping people and decided to help myself instead.

I studied and worked very hard. I worked my way up, job by job, until I was hired on my own merits by some of the richest men in the world. These moguls included the legendary Tiny Rowland, whom a famous Conservative MP once called, 'the unacceptable face of capitalism'. I also worked for a Japanese Samurai called Harunori Takahashi. He had a net asset worth of $30 billion and was the single largest foreign investor in most of the Pacific Rim countries. He was featured in a famous 60 Minutes program called 'Showdown with a Shogun'. Takahashi was one of the richest and most famous men in Japan, once described by Asia Magazine as 'the world's busiest man'.

I had made it. I was fabulously rich, wonderfully dressed and beautifully bejeweled. I had homes, vintage cars, famous friends and lovers. I had power, influence and all the trappings of material success. In terms of what society taught me to value, I had it all.

However, after a time, I became miserable. I didn't fit in.

The business world I moved in was about hostile mergers and acquisitions, dog-eat-dog exploiting, maverick behaviour that was often unscrupulous and at times totally corrupt. When I discovered all this, I wanted out. But I didn't want to give up my high living lifestyle. Since this included bills, mortgages and so many payments to make, I needed to continue earning vast amounts of money, and so I continued to do what I increasingly hated and loathed myself for doing. I was caught in the trap and saw no way out.

At that time, I felt listless, empty and drained. Friends directed me to Harley Street doctors who catered to the rich and famous. They supplied me with diet pills that both gave me extra energy and helped me to keep my skinny figure. When diet pills ceased to give me the lift I wanted, I moved on to illegal drugs, in particular cocaine. I became an addict and destroyed the high life I had built. Cocaine was costing me £500 a day by then. What friends failed to steal or embezzle from me, I spent on drugs. My house of cards gradually fell in on me. I just spent each day thinking of drugs and in a total agonized conflict... where 50% of my time was spent hating myself for being powerless over my addiction and wishing I could stop, and the other 50% was spent thinking, *how can I get MORE?*

So, I'd gone on an extreme binge that night and managed to kill myself. At last I was free of it all, or so I thought. There I was, on the floor, smelly, degraded, and dead. I looked down at the body in disgust.

Then I realized that an incredible sapphire blue light was glowing around me. I was aware that it was alive and conscious. I knew I was dead and so I thought the blue light was God or something. I felt overwhelmed by a feeling of light power and a love for me that was so pure it transcended anything I had ever felt.

At that time in my life, I didn't even believe in angels. In fact, it was a few days later before I learned the identity of this being. It was the Archangel Michael who had guided me through my life review and then he showed me what I was really supposed to do in this life. He told me it was not my time to leave and he sent me back, reborn, miraculously healed from the ravages of drug addiction.

Carrying this new light, I began the life of caring for and

helping others, teaching and healing them like I had dreamed of doing when I was a child.

Before I returned to my body, Michael gave me a telephone number. It was propelled into my mind, engraved there, and I knew it had to be important. When I regained consciousness I was on my bed. I felt incredibly euphoric. On the table next to me was a huge pile of drugs, but they no longer held any appeal. Then the number the angel had given me popped into my head. I felt my hand was being guided when I dialed it. It turned out to be that of a film producer friend, Trisha Shorten, who I had last seen in Los Angeles three years ago. We had lost touch and she had just moved back to South Africa. At the time, she was just the person I needed to see. She was very spiritual and really helped me overcome my weaknesses. People might say that I must have hallucinated the angel visitation, but I didn't hallucinate being given the phone number – it was ex-directory, and there was no way I could have got it for myself.

Things weren't changed quite like magic, but I learned how faith and trust can move mountains. I wanted to create something wonderful, a place for healing that would draw people from all over the world. My understanding that this creation was my very reason for being started an amazing procession of small miracles. People started to donate money to help me, and it was a case of 'if you build it, they will come'.

I built my place of healing in Wells near Glastonbury in Somerset and called it PSALM – PSA Life Mastery. And come they did, from all walks of life and all backgrounds.

Now, nothing of this material world holds any temptation for me. I've already had an excess of everything fame can give and fortune can buy. Instead, I have now truly found my path and live my passion. My message to you is that you too can live this completion of your dreams and have this happy ending with ongoing joy.

I learned to be grateful for each day I was clean and sober in the moment. At first if I bought something useful with my money, I'd automatically calculate how many drugs I could have bought with that money and feel wistful temporarily, then I'd pull myself together and renew my determination to stay in touch with my pain. After about nine months all the pain and shame the drugs suppress comes tumbling back into awareness, almost like giving birth to yourself again...and that's a very tough time for addicts because they feel euphoric in those first few months of clean time. However, when this dark night of the soul approaches, it's so overwhelming for many that they rush back to the drugs.

Luckily I found the right tools to deal with that crisis eventually. I discovered Reiki to balance and heal myself daily and this was, and still is an incredible tool. I adopted a shamanic approach to correct my mental and emotional problems called psychological recapitulation where I constantly worked with my shadow character defects to correct these in all my relationships with others and above all to myself. I learned to discipline my mental thoughts and to express my emotions healthily. This helped to stabilize me psychologically and worked as if by magic.

The harder I worked, the more powerful the resurrection was from the lead of personality (ego) to achieve spiritual gold. The angels *never* left me and introduced all kinds of spiritual guides and teachers.

As I learned to still my mind and keep my focus on love, my overall energy field purified and was quickened, then I was amazed to be able to see these invisible helpers regularly. Now in my trainings I teach others how to do this too.

My advice to any other addicts reading this is, never give up, and keep on keeping on taking each day in the day. The most important thing to realize is that addiction is not a disease. I know this goes against what modern medicine says. However, the inspiration I was given whilst fighting to stay free of addiction was this. Addiction is only a symptom of a much larger disease –

self hatred. It is self hatred in all its various forms, such as lack of confidence, lack of self esteem, valuing ourselves on external symbols of power, status, and things. Self hatred is the real disease, and the entire planet suffers from that when they are in separation from spirit and forget what the ancients call 'The Great Mystery'. It's only when we take time to stop our busy do/have/consume lifestyles and still ourselves that we can learn how to reconnect to spirit and find our best selves, live our best lives.

www.psalifemastery.com

This visitation not only saved Susie's life, and brought her back from the brink, it also gave her a way forward that changed her life and helped her to help others. This is the way to true happiness – being shown your master plan and being given the means to follow it.

*

Saved By an Angel

Jane Amber

It was January 2002 and I was feeling anxious and agitated. "Why?" I asked myself. I decided to do a month-by-month forecast with the tarot deck to see what the outlook for the year ahead was, but as I shuffled the cards and laid them out, an uneasy feeling washed over me. The Devil and Tower came up close together and my anxiety turned to dread.

I put the cards away and tried to get on with my day, but my mind kept drifting back to the tarot cards. Why was I feeling so afraid and what was coming up in the summer? The cards were clearly telling me that something was not right, a warning I suppose.

August came, and a friend of mine returning from her holiday invited me to meet up with her. She lived in central London, close to a major carnival that takes place each year, and coincidentally it was on the weekend that we had agreed to meet. So with the date fixed, my husband and I left to meet with her. I had been feeling uneasy all morning, but on the train to London, as we approached the stop, I began to feel even worse. Something was just not right. The air felt heavy when we got off the train, and I could feel fear around me. By 9.30am we had reached my friend's flat and we waited there until 11am, as more of her guests arrived. I was desperately trying not to show the anxiety and fear I was feeling, so as not to spoil the festive mood. Everyone else there was ready to party. How could I explain to them what I was feeling in my gut?

"Let's go!" my friend said. We could hear the carnival getting going to the sound of drums and loud music. It was time to join the crowds. I asked my husband to stay close to me as we walked towards the music in the street. I was surrounded by people wearing masks and lovely extravagant costumes but I simply could not join in the spirit of things. I can only explain what I felt as a dense energy surrounding me, which I could feel while those around me were unaware of it. Then, suddenly I felt a presence attached to my arm. As much as I kept brushing my arm to try to get it off, it wouldn't go away. It felt like when a fly lands on your skin, only bigger, much bigger.

I then began to see men in front of me, with hoods over their faces, and I felt terrified. This 'thing' stuck to me like glue, and the men in hoods became surrounded by a sea of white mist. The group of people that I was with wanted to get deeper into the crowds but I told them that I was feeling sick and asked for the keys to go back to the flat, telling them all to go and enjoy themselves and not to worry about me. The whole time I felt this 'thing' stuck to my arm, it was very real, and yet no-one else knew anything about it. I realized that I wasn't as much scared by this presence as perplexed by it. My real fear lay in venturing further into the carnival crowds.

I let myself into my friend's flat put the kettle on and walked over to the window to see what I could of the carnival, at which point I had a sudden inexplicable urge to jump out of the window. I was frantically trying to open the window without knowing why. I tried to lift up the sash and jump out, but some kind of 'energy' pulled me back with force. I ran into the bedroom and lay on the bed and as I looked at the wall the words 'SAVED BY AN ANGEL' appeared before my eyes in writing on the wall. I felt a huge sense of relief on seeing this, and yet utterly confused at the same time. Why did I want to commit suicide? I was happy, I wasn't depressed at all. What was going on? What was it that made me try to take my own life?

Some hours later my friend and her guests returned to the flat for a drink. I told them that I still felt sick and wanted to leave. I did not know what else to say. They would have thought I was crazy if I had told them what really happened to me. My husband and I left the flat and headed home. I could not wait to get away from the area. I still felt the presence of some kind of dark force. The following day I went to my local Spiritualist church to pray and to thank the angels for their help. As I sat down there was a gap between myself and another lady. I looked at the chair between us and on it was a book by a great author called 'Saved by the Angels'. This took my breath away. I felt that it was obviously meant for me to read. I was sure that I had just been saved by the angels.

The presence with me on that day I believe was a guardian angel attached to my side. I asked the lady if I could buy the book from her and we exchanged money straight away.

I feel that there was a warning in the tarot about that day also. A short time later when I arrived home I rang a policewoman friend of mine to tell her what had happened to me. I knew that she was spiritually aware so I could explain everything to her. She told me that she had been working at the carnival that day and that a woman had committed suicide by jumping out of the window of a flat. That could have been me, but I was saved by the angels. I have since qualified as an Angel therapist and teacher.

www.Janeamber.co.uk

What was this? Was there some kind of battle going on for Jane? Were the forces of good and evil lined up, with her in the middle? Something tried to make Jane kill herself, although she hadn't wanted to, and something else saved her.

*

Saved For My Children

Jacqui Grogan

When I was in my early twenties (in the 1980s) I hit a very low point in my life when the father of my children was sentenced to life for murder. I became ill all the time, and with two young children to look after I couldn't afford to give up on life as I had no family to support me.

Everyone vanished from our life or tarred us with the same brush as him. We had been sent to prison too, and my children felt the effect of his wrong doing, especially my son, as he looked like his father, and my daughter, who became angry and confused.

One day while I was lying in bed, suffering with yet another facial abscess the size of a football, I experienced my energy totally draining from me. I was riddled with extreme pain, and I had had no relief for what seemed like years and felt that I would be better off dead. I was in the depths of despair and assumed that life was just a living hell, and then something very spiritual and enlightening happened.

My body had become very light. I was up at the ceiling looking down. I witnessed my spirit leave my body, and everything around me was so peaceful and clear. I was hovering in the air above my body, watching my life fading away, yet I felt at peace. Everything was so bright, I felt free and a field of love was embracing me. I was so happy and Loved, I didn't want to return to the cruel world I knew...

Suddenly my children came running into my room after returning from school. I could hear them shouting "Mummy!" My heart strings were tugged and I could see their innocent faces. Who would look after them? It was only me that they had. Sadness filled my heart at the thought of no-one loving them as I do.

All of a sudden both fear and unconditional love grabbed hold of me, and I felt my spirit crash back into my body, bouncing back to life. Landing hard on the bed I became conscious of the life I had been so willing to leave behind. I couldn't believe what had just happened and had this voice of realization tell me that it was not my time to leave this place after all. I had a job to do, a mission to accomplish, I had to learn how to move on. I was not going to be beaten by someone who'd not only ruined the victim's family (in this case his own too) but left his mark on us as well, and the next generation of innocent bystanders. I decided to fight for our rights.

I later learnt that I'd had an out of body experience... and what a wonderful experience it was...

A few weeks after this incident, I was at the end of the corridor that led to my bedroom. I was still very low at this point and still so drained of life, wondering what other lessons I had to endure before life got better. I felt a strong presence watching over me and I looked up and saw this huge being of light. I felt overwhelmed. It must have been at least eight feet tall, I couldn't see any features as everything was so bright, yet so inviting. I could see a mass of light that appeared to be a figure and I was beckoned to come closer. It filled the whole place with a loving energy and told me that I was going to be all right. I was told I was here for a purpose and that purpose would be revealed to me in the future but I had many lessons to learn first. A few years later I found out that this guardian's name was Archangel Michael, who has been by my side all my life. He was the one who comforted and supported me through all the bad times, accidents and illness I had been through since childhood, and now he had shown himself to me.

After this visitation I started to receive many messages, through lots of channels including my art work. I had messages saying that I was here to help others heal, and had been given each lesson to learn so that I could understand first hand about compassion and how to be non-judgmental of others. But I had to learn how to heal myself first and return to my spiritual home... Love. I was told that I was a pointer, like John the Baptist directing others towards living in the light, rather than existing in the dark, my work was helping others bring their darkness into the light to be healed. I was also told I would be a greeter on the other side of the Golden Gate, once I had served my life's purpose.

Once the apparition of Loving light disappeared I was left with a great inner feeling of knowing that there is more to life than meets the eye. I had a job to do, and no matter how long I took, I would reach a point where I was returned to Love and all my life's experiences would become only a flicker of faint memories. Total healing began for me that day. And I thank God he was there to show me the way...

I have been visited by many Angels and Spirit Guides since, and am so grateful to them for blessing me with their presence.

http://www.edenspirit.co.uk

There's no doubt in my mind that angels can help us, but we have to ask them. There seems to be an unwritten rule that they can't intervene unless we call them. In Jacqui's case her subconscious was obviously crying out for help and an angel heard it.

*

My Grandfather

Greg Evans

One hot day in the 1970's when I was between nine and ten years old, I decided to leave the local park and get an ice-lolly. My friends didn't want to leave the park. It was a big play area with swings, slides roundabouts and large grass lawns that were enclosed by an iron fence and huge trees.

We called it the lollipop shop and it sold homemade 2p iced lollipops, and was just up the hill and across the road from the park. I rushed off alone for the shop with the 10 pence piece I'd got from my mother.

Unfortunately, as a child, I had a habit of putting everything in my mouth. On my way there I carried my coin in my mouth. I was puffing and panting from all the running around in the park, and suddenly the coin went down my throat.

I felt it slip down. I retched to get it up, but it only hurt my throat even more. I even tried to swallow it, but it was stuck fast in my windpipe.

I realized that I needed help. I was in the middle of the road, there were no cars and there were no people around. Nobody was there to help me.

I couldn't decide what would be quicker, to carry on to the shop or to go back to my friends. I just stood there in the middle of the road gasping for air. I knew that I wouldn't make it in either direction.

As I strained to get what little air I could into my lungs, a thought came into my head, *this is it, I'm going to die.* It was a calm thought as I accepted death.

The sense of calmness went over me like a wave, and then suddenly I felt a huge thump on my back. My body bent with its force and the coin shot out of my mouth and rolled across the road. I looked around to see what had hit me, but there was nothing there. No cars, no people. But I knew what the calmness was.

Being a young boy, I shrugged, casually retrieved the 10 pence and went to the shop for a lollipop. I told nobody about it, and particularly not my mother.

A few weeks later, I came home from school, and as always I was looking forward to tea and TV. I opened the door and immediately knew something was up.

My mother was sitting in a chair near the door, and two of her friends were standing next to her. They were all staring at me. All in total in silence.

Even at that young age I knew that when three women are joined in silence there was something going on. I waited to be accused of something that I hadn't done.

My mother asked in a no nonsense manner, "Did you nearly choke on a ten pence piece the other week?" I was ready to play the falsely accused, but that changed everything. I was caught out. I was never any good at lying and I knew that.

I replied, "Um, yes," thinking I'd get a stern lecture for the rest of the week.

Their faces had the look of shock. As if I'd said a naughty word.

I quickly defended myself, "I didn't though. I was all right." My mother interrogated me about the hows, wheres and whens, which didn't seem to ease their shocked faces, but only made them worse.

I sat on the settee and sulked. I knew that putting things in your mouth was a stupid thing to do. My mother came over to me and started to explain how she knew about the 10 pence. She said that while I was in school, she and the other two ladies had gone to a medium's house. It was my turn to be shocked. I had learned at an early age that the spirits that I encountered including my grandfather, who died when I was just under two years old, was best not mentioned to other people. My mother had heard restless spirits on occasions and seen what they can do with a 10ft bamboo pole, but that didn't make it an open subject. For once I was the listener and someone else was the teller. The skies opened up.

My mother said that the medium told her that her little boy was outside a park, choking to death on a 10 pence piece, which my mother had solemnly denied to her. Her little boy would tell her if it was true. She said that the medium persisted, and told her that her father was there (in spirit) and had slapped her son on the back, dislodging the coin and saving his life. When she finished telling me about what the medium said and had it confirmed by me, my mother asked me if I'd known my grandfather was there. I told her yes.

I believe that was the first step for my mother to accept spirits were real. After many bad episodes which get pushed out of peoples minds as hallucinations, this was the first good thing from a spirit she had proof of besides mine. It was a blessing to learn that when she wasn't around to help her son, her father was always available.

I loved this story. To see that our loved ones don't always cross over, but stay around to watch over us is such a lovely thought. The world would have been changed if the boy had died in so many ways too. All of these mistakes were repaired by his Grandfather's actions in saving him.

*

A Helping Hand

Linda Ferrier

I was only 12 at the time, and I'm 36 now, but I remember it as if it was yesterday.

It was a day at the beach, and nothing scary or dangerous was meant to happen. We'd been on the sand for a while and then the family decided to go for some lunch. In those days this always caused an argument because I was the only one in our big family who'd become a vegan. As always, the family wanted to get a burger or some disgusting reformed chicken stuff to eat, and if we followed their choice there'd be nothing I could have but a salad. They tried to talk me round, saying they'd find something more for me to have afterwards, but I was having one of those young girl strops, and I marched off in a hormonally charged huff. I can't even really remember why I got so mad now, it was all so silly, but I do remember what happened next.

As the family went off to the shops, I jumped back down onto the sand and started walking, climbing over the wooden breakers one by one until I was far enough from my family for the steam to have left me. What I hadn't realized, in my temper, was that the wall had gradually gotten higher and higher, and that the sea had gotten closer and closer.

When I came back to myself, the water was lapping only inches from my feet, and when I turned, my concern quickly changed to panic when I realized that the wall was way too high for me to climb back up to safety. I looked back the way I'd come, but I knew I'd never make it before the tide came right in. I looked ahead but that way the wall gradually joined the cliffs, and there was no way out.

What scared me more than anything was that I couldn't swim – not a stroke, and there was a strong wind coming in with the sea, and dark clouds overhead. Getting wet I could have coped with, but a cold hand clutched my heart because I just knew I was going to drown. I could almost taste the cold, salty water going into my mouth and down into my stomach and chilling me right through, as it cut off my breath.

I started to yell, "Help me! Someone help me!" But I knew that I'd gone so far from the popular end of the beach that there wouldn't be anyone there to hear me. By then my feet were wet and the water was up to my ankles.

Suddenly, I heard something above me. The wall was over six feet high, but there was someone up there. A face peered over the edge, a nice man's face, quite young, framed by unruly brown hair. He reached his arm down to me, "Need a hand?" he asked.

I reached up as high as I could and clutched his hand in mine, still scared because I didn't see how he'd have the strength to pull me up. But I was suddenly hauled aloft and was able to scramble to the top using rough stones as footholds. Next thing I knew I was sprawled on the pavement, feeling like I wanted to kiss it. I turned to the man, "Thank you so much…" on my lips. But I was talking to thin air. There was no-one right beside me and no-one anywhere along the deserted promenade. There was no building for half a mile in either direction, and nowhere else the man could have gone. He'd vanished as if he'd never existed. And yet, his hand had felt so solid in mine. I'll never know who he was, angel or ghost, but I'll never forget him.

My life almost ended at the very young age, and now I can't help but think of what I'd have missed, but for a helping hand. I wouldn't have been married; I wouldn't have given birth to my two wonderful children. So, that day, three lives were saved, not just one.

The superhuman strength this being showed, leads me to think that it was yet another example of someone in danger, crying out for help and having their angel help them, because it wasn't the right time for them to die.

*

My Wife, My Angel

John Brooks

The 28th of April 2006 started out like any other day for me. I gathered up my three year old son, packed him into the car and headed off from Laramie to Rock River. This was a 40 mile drive to the babysitter's to drop him off, and then on to work at 5:00 am. About half-way there the car's battery light came on, and then the engine began to shudder, as if all the spark plugs had been pulled out, and then the check engine light came on. I pulled over to the side of the road and popped the hood of the car to see what, if anything was wrong. I couldn't see any obvious problem so I decided to walk to the nearest house and use the phone to call someone to come get me. As I reached inside to pick up my son the car came back to life as if nothing had happened, so I jumped in and proceeded to drive the rest of the way to the babysitter's with no problems from my car.

About four miles out of Rock River I saw headlights bouncing across the median, so I slammed on the brakes, missing what turned out to be a semi, by just a few yards, as he stopped on my side of the road completely blocking both lanes of oncoming traffic. I jumped out and pounded on the door of the cab to see if the driver was alright, but no one answered, so I flew into town to the babysitter's (who is an E.M.T.) and told her what just happened. We called the police, and for ten minutes they asked for all the details. I then carried on to work.

The driver's story, he said, was that he remembers driving through Rock River and was becoming drowsy as he neared the park in the center of town, so he rolled down his windows to keep himself awake. As he passed the park he saw a woman waving her arms and yelling, "Don't hit my baby! Please don't hit my baby!"

He said he felt he should have stopped, but was running late so decided to carry on. The next thing he remembered was seeing a car in front of his truck, with a man driving, and a little boy in the car seat in back. Then he must have blacked out or something, because the next thing he remembered was the EMTs and the Sheriff pounding on his door, and he was asking, "Did I kill them? Are they all right?"

The babysitter who was one of the EMTs, told him that my son and I were fine, and that we were the ones who had called for help. The babysitter and the Sheriff both asked the driver if he could describe the woman who had shouted at him, and he told them that she had long dark hair, was wearing a black striped sweater with dark blue jeans. He described her face to them, and both the Sheriff (who knows us) and the babysitter, looked at each other in total disbelief. He had described my wife, who had passed away two years earlier to the day, and stranger still, he had also described the clothes she was wearing the day she died.

They came and told me later that morning, and the whole town was soon abuzz with the miracle of mine and my son's brush with death. I believe that my wife came back to save us from a certain death. Had she not caused my car to stall when she did we would have been a few seconds earlier to meet the truck and we would have died. She truly is an angel, as she always said that if she went before me she would make sure that my son and I would never be harmed until it was our time to go.

This story should bring hope and comfort to anyone who has lost somebody dear to them. It proves that death is not a closed door or even a barrier. Our loved ones still walk beside us for as look as we need them, or as long as they choose to.

*

The Angel in the Tree

James Coulbert

When I was about 12 or 13 years old, we went to go and see my Auntie who was at the time holidaying in a caravan in the middle of the New Forest in Hampshire, southern England. The location of the forest was not far away from where we lived, so it was just to go and spend the day with them. There was a great storm in 1987 which felled many of the great trees in the area. My cousins, siblings and I decided to climb this tree that was now lying on its side. Even though the tree was now lying on the ground, I realized that it must have been huge, because even navigating along the side of its trunk and then climbing the branches, I was still about 15 - 20ft above the ground. The others got bored quickly as I was good at climbing and they weren't so keen, so they all decided to leave the tree and go and do something else, so not wanting to get left behind I tried to get down as fast as possible.

This storm had happened about eight years before, so this tree's branches had been dead and exposed for almost a decade, and suddenly, because I was moving so forcibly through it, the bit I was moving along gave way and went crashing to the ground. To this day I don't know how I remained in that tree. The only feeling I can remember is the sensation of floating (not flying!) just being suspended there in the air. Even though I was still holding onto another branch with one of my hands, neither that branch, nor my upper body strength was enough to support all of my weight. I didn't even feel like I was dangling. After a few moments, my feet found a stronger branch and I carefully made my way back down to the ground.

I wasn't fully aware of what I really knew had happened, until much later on in life when I began researching about guardian angels after getting it into my head one day that I had one.

There is no doubt in my mind that my angel, whom I am now fairly sure is called Anna, came to my rescue and held me until she found a way of getting me to a safer part of the tree and stayed with me, guiding me until I got to the ground.

Anna is a big part of my life now and I frequently feel her, when she is next to me. It's not always necessarily in a time when I need her help, but it can just be when I'm reading something that moves me, or if I'm listening to a really beautiful piece of music, and then she'll just come and sit by me and I can sense that. Sometimes, when I'm driving, she'll send a bird to fly in front of my car and I'll know to slow down for whatever reason, usually for oncoming traffic, or a speed camera! I love Anna. I have yet to see her, and I live in hope that she is able to show herself to me one day, so that I can say thank you to her.

Once you connect with your angel in the way James did, and they show themselves so clearly, it seems there's no going back. What a wonderful way to live you life, so sure of your guardian.

Chapter Five

Babies have Power too

The most poignant of loses has to be that of a young child or baby. It never seems natural for a child to leave the world before their parent, but a very young one, barely setting foot on the Earth before leaving again, is particularly dreadful. How can anyone survive such a devastating loss? Here are some stories of babes who despite their young physical age, had tremendous spiritual energy and loved so much that they used this power to bring comfort to their grieving parents.

The White Baby Sock

Christine Potter

In 1999 I had the worst year of my life. My baby was stillborn. No-one can imagine what it's like to wait excitedly for nine months, feeling their baby grow and kick, to find out that it is a little girl, to paint the nursery, buy a pretty crib and tiny dresses, to be so expectant, only to lose the child before they even get to hold it in their arms.

After I was discharged from hospital, I would sit for hours in the nursery, listening to the musical mobile and watching the little carousel horses go round and round above an empty cot, which was just about as empty as my heart.

I had been going to call the baby Patience, as I had been trying for her for several years, always trusting that she would come one day. Now she had come, and gone, and I felt desperately cheated. I would sit and dream of her first words, her first day at school, her first boyfriend, her wedding, and grandchildren, only to come back to reality with a bang. It was never going to happen.

My depression was so deep that my husband and my Mum got very worried about me. The very worst thing was the people who dismissed my baby girl as having never really lived, and therefore not as important as one I would have 'had time to grow attached to'. Utter rubbish – I was as attached to my daughter as it was possible to be.

But they were right in a way, I had to get back to living my own life, so I did the dreaded deed and got rid of all the clothes and toys and furniture, crying all the time. I was criticized for that too, because they said I should have kept some of it for the 'next one'. This stuff belonged to Patience, not some future possible usurper of my affections. I really couldn't imagine ever loving another baby like I'd loved my Patience anyway. So it went, all of it.

We started trying for another baby, but it wasn't happening, even when I finally got to the stage where I really wanted it, I just couldn't get pregnant. It seemed that Patience had been my only chance at maternal happiness, and I got very depressed again.

Then one day I found something. A tiny, white, baby sock. It was in my dressing table drawer. The odd thing was that I don't remember ever putting it there. It wasn't as if it was a pair of socks. Why on Earth would I put just one sock in my drawer? I felt its presence was like a lucky charm put there by my baby's spirit. Whether I was right or not, it did work 'like a charm'. I put it under the pillow that night, and we tried again to get me pregnant. Believe it or not, the very next day I did a pregnancy test, and it was positive.

All through my pregnancy, the specter of the stillbirth of Patience haunted me, but so long as I had that little white baby sock with me, I felt safe. It never left me for the whole nine months, and when baby Patience finally made it safely into the world, I believed that my connection to her through her sock was what made it happen. I believe this little girl I now hold has the same soul as the one who died. And the sock? I still keep it with me. It's grubby by now and worn with handling, but I'll just keep it, because so long as I have it, Patience is safe…

This sweet story gave me goose bumps! I could feel Christine's pain and her joy now that she has her child safe in the world. I do believe this little soul is Patience come back, because no soul is ever lost and no connection is ever broken. I feel her first attempt at coming into this world failed because the world wasn't ready for her for some reason. Once the time was right, she returned.

*

I Had To Let My Daughter Die

Lucy Long

I had to let them kill my daughter. Well, that's how some people would see it. Cora was my little angel. She always wanted to be Mummy's helper, and you'd never find a child with a sweeter nature. As a tiny baby she'd rarely cried, rarely had a sniffle, and always been ready to chuckle. I'd tried to get pregnant for so long, having suffered from health and fertility problems, and then when Cora finally arrived she was the answer to all my prayers.

I can remember the moment when I did the pregnancy test and found out that against all the odds, I was carrying our child. It was a magical feeling.

We lived in France at the time, near Lyon, and the doctors told me I would never have another child, after the birth, but that was OK because Cora was all I'd ever wanted. My hubby Harry loved her to bits too, and he was a great Dad. I like to think we were both great parents. No little girl was ever loved more.

Two years ago, a week after Cora's fourth birthday, she seemed a bit off-color. Like any paranoid Mum would, I called the doctor. I speak fluent French, so there was no translation problem. He told me not to worry, there was a bug going round, and she'd probably picked it up at nursery school. That night she was so hot I got really scared. She started mumbling in her sleep, and her cheeks were really red.

My heart dropped like a stone when Harry found the rash on her arm. We did the glass-pressing test, and the rash didn't fade. In total panic, with the word 'meningitis' screaming in our heads, we rushed her to the hospital.

Three days later my world ended. Just three days turned Cora from a happy, wonderful, playful, light of my life, into a comatose child, on life-support, with no chance of recovery, the doctors said. Harry and I were totally devastated. We couldn't grasp how things could have gone so tragically wrong in such a short space of time. After a while the doctors wanted us to turn off the life-support. But how could we? We stood by her bedside watching the slow rise and fall of her little chest, knowing that a machine was doing that for her. Even though we knew she wasn't capable of breathing on her own, we couldn't bear the thought of giving up, of seeing her still, of knowing that she could never wake up again. The rise and fall of her chest mesmerized me as I just sat and stared at my perfect little girl. Day after day we stood there and night after night we lay in bed, failing to sleep, praying for a miracle.

I got one, of a sort. One night I fell asleep despite myself, and in the dream Cora came to talk to her Mummy. It was so real. I could touch her, feel her, hear her, and it was heartbreaking, because somehow I knew it was a dream. I could smell her sweet scent and feel the soft toweling of her pajamas. But even while she talked to me, and I smiled at her, I knew that in reality she was lying motionless, vegetable-like, in a hospital bed.

Cora's words cut so deep, "Mummy, please let me go," she begged.

"No, angel," I told her, "I can't."

Cora showed me some things.

On the one hand I saw her body, aged twenty years, still lying in a coma. Sixteen years, and she had never woken up, never moved, her body fed by tubes, and by then she was emaciated and pale.

On the other hand I saw Cora, running in fields, laughing and playing, and I knew she was showing me herself in spirit, as she would be, if I let her go.

There is nothing I wouldn't have done for my little girl, but this, what she asked me, was the hardest thing I could ever have imagined. I would have more easily died in her place.

The next day I talked to Harry, to discover that he had already resigned himself to letting her go, but he needed me to be ready too.

Together we kissed our baby goodbye. We stroked her hair for the last time, and held her little hands in ours. She was warm, breathing, and it was so awful to nod to the doctors. That little assent was telling them to turn her cold and lifeless.

Slowly her breathing stopped. She was still. She was gone. I turned and ran from the hospital, poor Harry was calling to me, but I had to be alone.

At the funeral I was in total shock, watching the too, too, small coffin being placed in the ground. Just weeks ago Cora had a future, and so did I. Now I was sentenced to a life with no child. I felt so empty and worthless. I really didn't know if I could go on. Life became one never-ending journey of despair.

After a year Harry persuaded me to have some more tests, and I agreed, for him, but I only had one working ovary, and such a damaged womb from endometriosis, that they said there was nothing they could do. The odds against us having a child were astronomical. We decided to move back to England, even though I felt like I was abandoning my little girl, leaving her alone in France. I felt we were moving further away from her – leaving her behind. Harry thought we'd recover better among our family in Lancashire.

I couldn't seem to get over the loss. I smiled on the outside, but inside I never stopped crying, never stopped seeing her face, I never stopped seeing her playing. I felt like I was slowly but surely dying, and part of me was glad. If I died maybe I'd get to see her playing and laughing again.

Then six months ago I had another dream.

Cora came to me again and told me, "Mummy! I'm going to come back to you!" She was excited, happy. It was so real. I woke up crying, and then cried even harder when I realized that it had just been a dream. I couldn't have another child. The doctors said so.

But, I was to learn that my little angel in heaven had more power than them. Two month later I missed a period. Elated and terrified I took a pregnancy test. I was pregnant. Harry and I were beside ourselves with joy. I didn't tell him my thoughts, as I wanted to be sure.

But last week I had a scan, and I'm carrying a little girl. It's a miracle, all the doctors say. It *is* a miracle, but one created by an angel. My little girl is coming home, and I can't wait!

I cried reading this, as you probably did too. This little soul loved her Mum and Dad so much that she was prepared to go through her illness and come out the other side. The reason for this? Who really knows? But there is no doubt that the death of a child changes people, and makes them see the world.differently. Perhaps this is the reason.

*

Still Born and Still Here

Diana Gardner-Williams

Me and my husband, Todd, arrived at our favorite mountain cabin Christmas Eve 2003. The cabin has a kitchenette, loft, cable TV, and indoor Jacuzzi tub. The back deck overlooks a steep, wooded hill with a pleasantly loud, rushing creek, barely visible through the trees. The evergreen shrubs flanking the entrance of the cabin were twinkling with multicolor lights, and a holiday mug filled with candy was centered on our kitchen table, welcoming us.

Since we usually spent Christmas with our family, we'd been unaware of the charming decorations provided by the owners at this time of year. So why were we there? The fact that our beautiful baby boy was born quiet and stillborn brought us to the cabin in the mountains. This was where we'd spend our first Christmas without our baby.

I'm originally from Buffalo, NY. I moved to North Carolina to study landscape architecture and decided to make my home here. The weather was more conducive to my career choice. I also met my wonderful husband Todd, there and we married in 2000. It wasn't until 2002 that we decided to expand our family. For some reason I changed my mind from May 2002 to August 2002 trying for a baby. I have always been a very planned and organized individual and thought having birthday parties in spring would be ideal. There would be an explosion of flowers, no mosquitoes, and the weather would be tolerable. After six long months of charting and taking my temperature, we finally saw two pink lines. It was apparent that I could not plan when my baby would be born. Our child was scheduled for a fall arrival, another favorite season of mine.

It was a very exciting time for us because several of our friends were also pregnant. The excitement faded for a while because morning sickness lasted into the night. I never actually threw up, and maybe hurling my cookies would have lessened the discomfort. Constant nausea made me unpleasant to be around. It wasn't until week 12 that the morning sickness passed and I was scheduled to see the doctor. At the appointment I was able to see the little heartbeat for the first time and wow, it was amazing. That little organ was created by us only three months ago. Me and baby were given a good report and were scheduled to see her in two more months, hopefully to find out the sex.

My friend and her husband owned their own sonogram machine, so I knew we would find out the sex beforehand. Todd and I anxiously drove to their office when I was 15 weeks along to see our little baby. Unfortunately we couldn't see the sex, but we did see a very active child. The entire 30 minutes was on tape and I couldn't wait to show family members what a beautiful child we had.

My husband came with me to the doctor's appointment where we would find out if the little one would wear blue or pink. I was very nervous because both my mother and mother-in-law had expressed their hopes for a little girl. We didn't care either way, but secretly I was hoping for a boy. We stared at the monitor like two kids staring at a glass candy jar. We could see that something was in there that we wanted, but the packaging camouflaged what it really was. Then the doctor pointed toward the screen to a white, opaque section. It was Tanner's penis. There is was, so tiny and the affirmation we were waiting for. We were thrilled, blue, blue, and more blue. Tanner would be my parent's third grandson, and my mother-in-laws first grandbaby. I know they were somewhat disappointed, but loved him regardless.

It seemed like the entire pregnancy was moving from one ailment to the next. The first three months it was the nausea, and then it was the round ligament stretching and finally the severe backaches. Towards the last few weeks I endured horrible indigestion and bruised ribs from Tanner's kicks. Truthfully, I did not enjoy my pregnancy and I couldn't wait to have him out.

I would later find out that I had stage four arthritis in my knees, and carrying extra weight had added to the stress. I would definitely take a rest from being pregnant after Tanner was born, so my body could heal. Tanner was due to arrive October 14th. However, on my husband's birthday I started having contractions that were closer together. I had bought Todd a gift and decided to let him open it in case this was the day Tanner would come. The contractions by then were less than two minutes apart, so I had Todd call the doctor for guidance. We were instructed to come in for a check. I called my best friend Evelyn to come over and join us at the hospital. My bags had been packed for two months and everything was in its place, so we easily slipped out of the house in a timely fashion at 2am. I was so excited and felt in my heart Tanner would be born on Todd's birthday.

The hospital was incredibly quiet and still as we checked in. Quickly we were led to a small examining room to check the progress of labor. I undressed and lay on the table while Todd stood by my side like a proud father to be. My cervix was still closed, but I was obviously having contractions. The ultrasound technician rolled her machine beside me and poured the cold lubricant on my belly. For some reason there were more nurses in the room now and the technician just stared at the monitor expressionless. Another nurse put an oxygen mask on my face and I was horrified. Finally someone said that the baby was probably hiding and giving me oxygen might increase his activity. That never happened. After seeing panic in my eyes, Todd asked if Tanner was moving. The technician kept her eyes on the monitor and said "No, I'm sorry."

At that moment I entered into another world that was so unfamiliar to me. This was a place that I had no control over and I could not plan my next move. This world would move me along on my journey not knowing what I would face next. I have never felt pain, loneliness and the need to grasp for air like this in my life. Could this be real? We held him, kissed him and loved him, but where is he? We would never be the same. We did expand our family, but instead of having a living son, we had a beautiful angel named Tanner.

We were inundated with information on how to survive the first year. Most of the bereavement books and literature suggested taking time for ourselves and gracefully decline family gatherings until we were more comfortable. That is exactly what we decided to do. Thanksgiving was spent at a friend's home and for Christmas, the two of us drove to our favorite mountain cabin in Spruce Pine.

I packed the candles, a lullaby CD, pictures of Tanner, and everything else reminiscent of him to create a shrine. I just wanted to think and feel everything about him during our stay. My eyes were so sore and red from crying so much.

Todd suggested that we get some fresh air and drive into the city of Ashville to shop. On our way to town I told Todd that I was upset that there were so many signs of Tanner, but none for us. The bear that played Ave Maria, the street sign 'Tanner Williams', the parent yelling for 'Tanner' at the park. Being his parents, I couldn't understand why we weren't given any signs from him. I told Todd, "I want my big sign!"

We spent several hours in town and the weather was gorgeous. I remember the quaint shops and brick laid alleys adding to its charm. The sun sets very fast in the mountains, so we headed back to our cabin around 5pm. The interstate speed limit is 70 miles per hour and I am glad that there wasn't much traffic at this time. Staring out of the window something caught my eye. My heart started to flutter and the palms of my hands were dripping with sweat. I was briefly in shock and had to snap out of it fast to tell Todd to pull over and stop. There it was, so high in the sky that I could not possibly miss it. The billboard read "TANNER". The hair on the back of my neck stood on end, and Todd sat quietly gazing at the grandiose sign. I quickly searched for the camera to take a picture, just in case it disappeared in a flash. After sitting on the side of the road for ten minutes we slowly drove off.

We were meant to see that billboard at that precise time in our lives. The sequence of events played a perfect harmony. We were there because of Tanner, and he blessed us with one of the biggest signs available to man. Seeing the billboard gave us so much hope and joy to keep going. Feeling his presence at just the right time spoke worlds to me. Our son being born quiet and still puts life in a much different perspective for me. I now view our time here as just a stepping stone. I truly believe we will all be together again and Tanner's beautiful song will keep playing for me until I can hold him forever.

This touching story is about a Mother who has realized that her baby came to her for a reason, and left for a reason. I'm sure that this understanding and love will bring to two of them together again when the time is right.

*

Twins Are Forever

Karen Samuels

I've always been open to the 'other side', because I've been there, having 'died' and been brought back to life by doctors, and it was this openness that allowed me to finally be reunited with the daughter I thought I'd lost forever.

When I was pregnant I'd been certain that I was carrying twin girls, because it had always been predicted by psychics. I'd been told I was to have one son and two daughters. I'd had the son, Rhys, and now I was expecting twin girls. But I should have been expecting trouble, because my own twin sister was lost during our mother's pregnancy.

Despite my strong connection to the two little souls inside me, when it came to my giving birth, there was only one baby. The only sign that there had been two of them was the large size of the placenta. The midwife was quite alarmed by it, because she said that it was too big for just one baby, and was the right size for twins. It was whisked away and tested, but still, there was only one baby, and I was told that the second one must have died and been reabsorbed. This confirmed my feelings, and I believed that I *did* have two daughters, but had lost one of them.

So I had to adjust. It was very hard because I'd even chosen names for the two babies. We called the daughter I gave birth to Siân.

My husband Gareth and I tried for another baby for a while but I developed a huge fibroid and a large ovarian cyst and had to have surgery. They wanted to remove everything but I declined as I wanted at least the chance to have another baby, but sadly, it never happened. Finally, I started to feel it wasn't to be, and as I was already older than most other mums of toddlers I stopped trying. I had my son, Rhys, and now I had a beautiful daughter, Siân, too.

I still wondered about where the other twin girl might be, and often talked to family when the subject came up. I remember saying, "I wish someone would put my mind at rest. If my third child is in spirit, then I can get used to it and get on with my life, instead of always wondering." I watched my two beautiful children grow, with pride and joy, and only occasionally wondered how it might have been if I'd had the three babies, as I'd always thought I would.

When Siân was nine years old, everything changed. I was having a reading from a psychic, who didn't know anything about me, not even my real name. I was amazed and delighted when she told me that I had a little spirit girl of nine years old, following me. But then the goose-bumps really started because she described the little girl to me in great detail. Every tiny thing she said made me realize that the description exactly matched Siân. Tears filled my eyes. The daughter I'd lost nine years previously had come back to me.

The psychic described the little girl's personality, saying she was very shy and quiet, quite the opposite to her living sister, Siân, who is cheeky and independent.

After that I was told that now I knew of my other daughter, she would come to visit us all at home. The little girl also made a poignant request. She asked if her Mummy would give her a proper name, just like her sister had. I named her Cerys, which had always been the name we would have given her if she'd been born.

Cerys started visiting often. The first time it happened was during a meditation. I saw a little girl shyly approaching me, carrying some marguerite-type daisies to give to me. In the first few seconds of seeing her I was terrified. She looked so much like Siân that I was afraid something might have happened to my living daughter, and that I was seeing her ghost, but I soon realized that the child standing before me was not Siân, but Cerys. She often talks to me now, telling me that she loves us all. She also protects her twin sister, accompanying her when she goes horse-riding. She once told me that she'd visited my Mum, and said that she'd been crying. It was on the anniversary of my Dad's passing, which is always a sad time for my Mum.

Cerys appears to us as a misty shape in Siân's bedroom, and we often hear Siân talking and playing with someone in her room, only to discover that she is alone. Now when I hear the two girls talking, I just listen, and it fills me with happiness to hear how close they are. In the middle of the night Siân's mechanical toys sometimes start up on their own even though she is asleep, and when the room's empty we hear little Cerys playing and laughing in there. Siân says she is very happy to have her sister come and play with her, and always includes her in their birthday celebrations.

One day Gareth was having a nap upstairs. He was woken by what he thought was Siân, telling him supper was ready. He followed the little girl downstairs and she disappeared into the kitchen. But when he came into the room I told him that Siân had been with me the whole time. When he realized that he had been personally visited by Cerys, his other little girl, he was delighted.

http://www.karenskreations.co.uk

This poignant little story speaks for itself. It seems that Cerys has decided to stay in the spirit world and grow up there. It could be that she knows she can be of more help from there than in the physical. I hope that Siân will always treasure the twin sister she has growing alongside her.

Chapter Six

Angelic Messages

Every culture in the world believes in angels in some form or another. Many people have encountered beings they believed were angels throughout history. Iin the 1700s Emanuel Swedenborg said, "There appeared to me very beautiful rainbows as on former occasions, but still more beautiful, with the light of the purest white, in the center of which was an obscured earthly something, but that most lucid snow white appearance was beautifully varied by another lucidity. And if I rightly recollect, with flowers of different colors round about."

His words come close to describing the rapture that's felt in the presence of one of these heavenly beings. There are many angelic encounters to choose from, but the ones that follow are some of the most beautiful I came across.

Angel or Vigilante?

Cassie Williams

I was driving home through the rain of a Kentucky winter night. My friend Alex was with me, and we were pretty nervous, two women driving alone through pretty empty countryside. There were no street lamps and the cloudy sky had totally blacked out any light from the moon or the stars. Beyond the beams of our car headlights there was nothing. Finally, to our relief we came to an all-night truck stop. (Thank God for the guys who man those godforsaken places!) We decided to stop, refresh ourselves and maybe even wait there until dawn. We'd both feel more confident traveling in daylight. I decided to call my Mom and tell her we'd be home later than we'd said. We were going to visit because my

Dad was ill, and I hadn't seen him for months.

Anyway, as soon as Mom answered the phone I knew something was badly wrong. "Cassie," she said, before I could tell her we were scared, "You'd better get here as soon as you can."

My heart stopped with those words. It turned out that Dad's pneumonia had brought on a heart failure, and they weren't sure how long he might have. We had no choice; we just had to get going, despite our trepidation. But, as luck would have it, we were made to feel even worse.

The waitress, asked us if we 'girls' were travelling alone, and when we said yes, she told us, "You'd be better to wait for daylight. We have a rapist on the loose around here. He's raped three women at the interstate rest room area. One woman was even killed by him."

We told her, we had to leave, or I might not be able to say goodbye to my Dad. She answered grimly, "Well don't say I didn't warn you. If you're not lucky you could be seeing your Dad afore you thought. On the other side."

I was determined to carry on, and for miles and hours I did. Then while we drove along the interstate I started to feel really sleepy. It was 3am by then, and I hadn't slept for 24 hours, since we'd had the first call about my Dad that had started us on this journey. I shook Alex awake and told her she had to stay awake to stop me falling asleep. She nodded drowsily, and for a while we were fine. If she saw my eyelids drooping, she'd start singing, and we wound down the windows. But soon she fell asleep again, and so did I. I woke up to see a stopped truck's taillights far too close for comfort. I slammed on the brakes and the car fishtailed on the wet road. The car shuddered to a halt. Alex, rudely awakened, said, "Oh Cassie, this is too bad. We have to stop. Imagine how bad your Mom would feel if she lost you...as well as your Dad."

She was right of course, we had to stop, just for an hour or two until it got light. It was no surprise to me, the way my luck had been going lately, to discover that we were approaching the very rest area that the waitress had warned us about. But we figured I had more chance of killing us in the car, than just happening to come across the rapist, so we pulled in, locked the doors, shut the windows, curled up, and closed our eyes.

I was just falling asleep, totally at that point where there is no turning back, when I realized that there was a figure looking in at me. Lit up by the nearby lamp, this man was very tall, very broad, and wearing a jogging suit. He had real blond hair, long and glinting in the light. He was peering into the car through the windshield. Weird as it might sound, I wasn't scared. It crossed my mind that it was a little weird for him to be wearing joggers in the pouring rain, and even more that he didn't appear to be wet. I just couldn't wake up, and I just thought, *I hope you're my guardian angel and not the rapist.* I heard a voice in my head say, "Your Dad will be fine. Sleep."

When we woke at first light, I didn't really remember what had happened. I just felt much happier and not so scared for my Dad. We drove on, and two hours later, we arrived at the hospital. Mom was ecstatic, and told me that Dad had pulled through after all, and she hoped I hadn't driven too fast!

I only remembered the strange man several days later, when I read the report of a local woman, who lived near to the rest area, who, after working nights had fallen asleep on her couch, instead of making it to bed one night. As she drifted off, she'd seen a big blond man, wearing joggers standing in her yard, looking in through the glazed kitchen door, and although she realized she's stupidly not locked her door, she just found herself unable to wake up. Hearing a voice in her head, saying, "I'll watch over you. Sleep." Thinking, *I hope you're my guardian angel and not the rapist,* she fell asleep for hours.

Was this an angel, or some kind of vigilante, protecting woman from the rapist. I'll never know for sure, but I have a good idea!

I have a good idea too, for how could a vigilante possibly know which women were going to be at risk? And how would he stop them waking up and being afraid of him?

*

A Test of Faith

Mary Hykel Hunt

Angels exist. They are real, living entities who are here to help and guide us.

I know this is true, because one came to meet me, one dark night, when I was about to lose my beloved Dad. He was lying in a hospital bed, very ill, paralyzed, and resigning himself to dying. He was 70 years old and was suffering from heart failure following a triple bypass. I was lying awake in my own bed at home at about 2am, choked with the pain of the impending loss. I somehow wrapped up all the pain into a ball of agony, and sent it out into the universe as a silent and desperate scream for help, as so many others have done before me.

Quite suddenly, a 'Being' appeared at the foot of my bed. It was about 9ft high, and massively winged, with flowing white hair and robes. It was clearly benign, but nevertheless exuded great power and strength. It stared at me and asked what I wanted. Surprisingly under the circumstances, I didn't bat an eyelid. Whatever this was, I just knew it could help. I said, "Please – help my Dad."

The Being nodded, and brought its enormous wings forward into a cradle shape. And there, held in those strong wings, appeared my Dad.

The Being looked at me again, and said once more, "What is it that you want?"

Feeling that somehow I was being tested, I responded, "Please

– I just want what's best for my Dad."

The winged Being looked hard into me and said, "You do know what that could mean?"

After a short pause, I answered with, "Yes – I do."

And I did. I knew that what was best for my Dad might be his release into death, and if that was the case, I would accept it for his sake.

At that, the entity nodded once more, turned gracefully, and carrying my father in the cradle of his wings, glided away through the wall.

I was awake for a very long time after that, checking myself out, making sure I had been awake and hadn't been dreaming. I was convinced that I would soon get the news that my Dad had passed away.

I didn't get a call, but sure enough, the following day, when I went back to my Dad's hospital bedside, I found the bed empty. I faltered and felt tears start to trickle down my face – my Dad had gone.

And then from behind me came a voice, "Hello, Mary. What are you doing here so early?" And there was my father, sitting upright in his chair, alive, back in himself. Far from being paralyzed as I last seen him, he was vital, alive and vibrant. I was overjoyed and ecstatic, both at his recovery and at this confirmation that the angel had been real.

That morning Dad had shocked and surprised the nursing staff, who had not been expecting him to last the night, by walking unaided to their station. They dubbed him the Miracle Man, because Dad made a full recovery and lived to enjoy five more years of good health, traveling and enjoying life.

It took me some while to pluck up the courage to tell Dad my version of the angelic intervention, but when I did, he showed no surprise at all, saying, "That night, at around 2am, a strange feeling swept over me. I realized that I was being offered a choice; to stay or to go. I thought about it, and decided to stay."

When Dad did pass away years later, I was able to contact him and be assured that he was still around and still able to guide me. I also made contact with my own guardian angel, Tobias, who's here to help and guide me on a daily basis.

Tobias is no saint. There's not a wing or a feather in sight. He wears Doc Marten boots, Wrangler jeans, and a chambray shirt, has shoulder-length black hair and thinks he's really cool. I've come to realize that I'm not dealing with an idealized Being here; I'm dealing with a real entity, with a life and thoughts and feelings of his own. He's here to help me. But that doesn't mean he obeys my every whim. He's here as a teacher. For example, one of the things he teaches me is there is a *right* time for things to happen, which can be wildly different from the time by which *I* want them to happen. This is difficult for me, because I am by nature an impatient person. I want things three weeks ago. But Tobias shows me that the *right* time runs to Heaven's schedule, not mine.

Of course, there are other things that Tobias does. He protects me. When I'm traveling, something I do often, I sense he's there, guiding me, protecting me. He took the wheel the other day when my car went into a skid. I didn't know what to do in that split second of slide, but *something* took over and guided the car to a safe standstill. On a roundabout, in the midst of heavy traffic, I glided to an elegant halt, admittedly facing the opposite way, nose to nose with an articulated truck, the bulk of which, interestingly, protected me from all the other vehicles that could have hit me.

You too can have access to this kind of help and protection, because one of the things I've discovered in my exploration into angels is that every single one of us has a Daily Angel, a guide who's there to help every one of us in every aspect of our life, big and small, crisis or everyday event.

We just need to learn to make that connection; to trust it, and the Being on the other side of it. I spend my time helping people to do just that.

http://www.hykelhunt.co.uk/

How interesting to read a description of an angel that differs so much from the classic picture we all have of flowing robes, white wings and holy attitudes. I feel that angels can appear to us in any form they choose, often to accommodate what they know we will accept. I once knew a child who saw her angel as a beautiful winged Unicorn, and why not?

*

A Mysterious Visitor

Jen Fowler

A while ago I was sitting on the sofa one night on my own, kids asleep and hubby out, watching TV minding my own business (as you do), when something caught my eye in the doorway towards the hall.

There was a man standing there. He was engulfed in a golden cloak of feathers and bathed in a beautiful light. He seemed almost too big to fit inside the doorway, and yet he did (or maybe that was his presence). He had beautiful shoulder length flaxen hair. I felt no fear. I watched him, entranced, for about five minutes, but funnily enough I didn't get up, or feel scared. All I felt was a beautiful sense of peace all around.

I call him my angel as that is what I thought he was. His image faded away slowly and didn't suddenly disappear, but once he was gone the feeling of peace remained.

Moving on to a few weeks ago, it was in the morning and I woke to find my husband had taken the kids down stairs to let me lie in (bless him). About quarter of an hour later he brought me up a cup of tea, and then left me to relax.

All of a sudden in broad daylight a beautiful rainbow aura

appeared in front of me, filled with what I can only describe as cherubs, with white wings. They were faceless, though yet again I felt the same feeling of peace wash over me, and it was the most beautiful image I had ever seen.

These images are still so vivid in my mind down to every little detail, even now.

So, here we have two very different angel appearances. One the classic winged being, and the other also classic in the shape of cherubs.

Chapter Seven

Synchronicity

Is there any such thing as coincidence? My following contributors would say a resounding 'no!' It's just a question of recognizing the synchronistic character of what some people would label pure coincidence. The Universe has a pattern and one of the ways of recognizing and interpreting that pattern is to recognize and interpret the little signposts that are dotted around our lives, if we're not oo blind to see them.

A Wash Out

Sally Thompson

I had often heard the word 'synchronicity', but never really knew what it meant until one day last summer. I have never been a believer in what I call *weirdities*, and never even read horoscopes, but then something happened which made me change my mind. After that I started reading a magazine called *Chat it's fate*, and realized I had something to share with the believers.

The most extraordinary day of my life started as soon as I woke up on 30th July 2003. The alarm rang and after slapping it off, I reached across to get a drink from the glass of water that stood on my bedside cabinet, and it just spun out of my hand and dropped to the floor. The weird thing was that the water didn't hit the floor, it splashed all over me, and the glass was practically dry as it landed on the carpet. Very odd I thought, and then I forgot about it, as you do.

The plumber was coming early to fit our new bathroom suite, so I got ready quickly, and didn't really notice that the shower was more difficult to control than usual, and zapped me in the face an extra number of times. Then the hose came off the tap and water squirted all over the place, soaking my hair, which I hadn't intended to wash. Most annoying.

The plumber arrived, and I wasn't that surprised somehow when everything went wrong. He thought he had turned off the stopcock, but when he disconnected the tap, water shot out, and, you guessed it, I was soaked through yet again! I started to joke about it, phoning my Mum and telling her, *somebody's trying to tell me something!*

By late afternoon the new bathroom was finished, and I was so pleased I forgot all about the many times I had been sprayed with water unexpectedly that day.

I decided there was still time for a bit of retail therapy, so I grabbed my bag, shut the front door behind me, and headed off to the shops. I knew it had been raining pretty hard all day, but I was a bit shocked went I stepped in what looked like a shallow puddle next to my car door, and my foot dropped with a splat into quite deep water. It splashed all over my legs and even made the bottom of my skirt wet. Darn it! My leather shoes were all soggy, but I glanced at my watch and thought that if I went back in to change I wouldn't get to the shops in time. At that point I almost decided not to go, but I was in gear, ready to shop till I dropped, and I pictured myself going back indoors with nothing to do, and didn't like that idea at all, so I got in the car. Sometimes we just don't listen do we?!

Anyway I drove off. I had been concentrating so much on the new bathroom all day that I really hadn't realized just how bad the weather had become. It was windy and chilly – British summertime, right? We lived about 12 miles out of town, down some narrow countryside roads. Our lane actually had quite a few potholes in it, and I had to dodge them carefully, because some of them would be quite deep under the puddles. The short route to town took me across a ford in the village, and although the water was running quite quickly I wasn't worried. I must have driven across it five or six times a week for the past three years. My car whooshed happily through the water. The trees along both sides of the lanes were swaying merrily, top-heavy with their summer leaves, and they did concern me a bit, but I was soon out of the lanes and onto the proper roads, so I carried on regardless. I soon reached town safely and set about spending some of my hard-earned cash.

I was laden with shopping and on my way back to my car when the water-demon struck again. I couldn't believe it! This complete idiot hurtled past me in his car, totally ignoring the fact that he was passing through huge amounts of surface water, and covered me all down one side with dirty puddle rainwater! The air was blue there for a while.

This next part was a bit spooky and I have to admit it freaked me out. As a car flashed away through the rain I saw his number plate. I couldn't see it that clearly, but it seemed to be DR 0VN. It was so close to DROWN that it made me gasp. But, like I said, I didn't believe in any of this stuff. It must be the same sometimes for people who see ghosts or something. They don't want to look stupid, so they talk themselves out of it, and that's what I did, and I laughed at myself and carried on. After all, I might have got wet several times that day already, but I hadn't exactly come close to drowning had I?

I got back to the car and thought to myself that I wouldn't get wet any more that day. I just wanted to get home. I was tired and hungry and well-satisfied with the bargains I'd found.

It had finally stopped raining, so I decided to take the short-cut. It would take me across the ford. If you're wondering, it *did* cross my mind. Ford – more water. But I refused, absolutely refused to take it seriously. I mean really, how stupid would I have to be to take another route home, just because of some 'coincidences'?

When I reached the ford I was a bit surprised. Normally, once it stopped raining, the fact that we were high up meant that the water level soon dropped, but on this day there was a bit of a raging torrent flowing. But, it didn't look any worse that in past times. I was stubborn.

It's funny, but on comparing my story with other peoples' I found that this is a common reaction to something 'otherworldly'. We dig our heels in and refuse to lose our logic.

I sat there in the car for a bit, and told myself that I was being silly to even hesitate. I was sure the water was no worse than before, and it would have taken me ages to go round the other way. I put my foot down and edged forwards, keeping the revs up as usual, so that the engine wouldn't stall if I got water up the exhaust pipe. I breathed a sigh of relief as I realized that the water wasn't too deep. The car felt fine as we chugged across. But suddenly the engine stopped. I turned the key, but the engine just sputtered and wouldn't catch. I thumped the wheel in frustration. I tried the engine again and again, sure that a farmer would happen by in his tractor (funny how tractors are always in front of you when you're in a hurry, but when you really need one, there are none to be found.)

That was when it happened. I had a sudden vision in my mind's eye of my car getting hit by a wave of water and carried away. I could see my terrified face looking out of the window as the car spun down-river.

It was like I suddenly woke up. All the signs I'd had all day rippled through my mind like a pack of playing cards, and I realized that they were warnings! Not coincidences at all. Without another thought I threw open the car door and plunged into the knee-high water. I shut the door behind myself out of sheer habit and staggered across to the other side. It was a bit slippery and the water dragged at my legs but I made it. As I reached dry ground I heard a terrible noise. It was water, lots of it, moving very fast. I turned around just in time to see a surge come around the bend. It hit the sides of the river and rebounded, crashing across the ford, at about shoulder height. In front of my shocked eyes, my Ford Fiesta was picked up as if it weighed just a few pounds and literally thrown into the river. It turned and twisted, half-submerged, and the only difference to my vision was that because of the warnings I'd had, there was no terrified face peering out of it.

I had been saved by *coincidences*, and from that day to this I have *never* ignored synchronicity.

A salutary warning to us all. If something seems too difficult and if obstacles keep jumping in the way, then somebody probably IS trying to tell us something! The next story confirms this very forcefully.

*

Haunted – by Bicycles?

Jill Wood

I've been a freelance writer for over twenty years, and for the past couple of years I've enjoyed holidays that I've converted into earning opportunities by writing for travel operators like Airtours. I've also written some fictional stories, and I always like giving readers 'posers', starting a story that is compelling most of all because they want to find out what on earth is going on!

My fifteen minutes of fame came when I appeared as an extra on Coronation Street. I've flown on a sky-dive simulator, commentated at Doncaster Racecourse, abseiled off a building, driven a lorry, and ridden a camel.

I've been on what I call my path to psychic awareness for some time, and every now and then I get a real kick up the rear, which makes me sit up and think. Intuition, awareness, it's all very important to us as we make our way through life – and sometimes it can even *save* our lives. I'm always on the lookout for signs and signals. Synchronicity is something I live by on a regular basis, but even I was astonished the day I was 'haunted' by bicycles!

I had gone with my friend and neighbor Jo to an alternative health clinic. We'd been friends and neighbors for a while, sharing chats and helping each other with her twin girls and my son, Mic.

Jo had decided to take the alternative medicine route because she was at the end of her tether with conventional medicine. I'd gone with her to give her moral support; otherwise she might not have gone. It was a good job she did, because she has made an almost complete recovery from her illness by the time of writing this.

The alternative health clinic was set in an old terraced house. Certificates in every therapy lined the walls, and the smoke from combusting Chinese herbs filled the atmosphere, as the physio-therapist turned healer went from room to room attending to her elderly patients. There was at least one treatment couch in every room of the house, with a patient on each, and another gently-smiling patient sitting on a nearby comfy chair. So popular is this clinic that she's always booked up, and we were glad to be able to get in and see her.

We'd been given a lift to the clinic, and we decided that we'd go home by train and then walk the rest of the way home, to get some fresh air. We only just caught the train home by a whisker, and of course timing is *everything* with synchronicity! After getting off the train at our home town we came up the steps to the station exit and set off down the road for home. As we walked along the busy main road, we were both shocked to see a very young boy pedaling along on a bike, with a toddler riding in front of him, standing up on the pedals. The two children and their bike were going at some speed, wobbling slightly in the downdraft from the convoys of huge articulated trucks that were whooshing past them. Other fast traffic was hurtling past too, and we couldn't believe what we were seeing. As mums ourselves, we couldn't believe that the boys' parents would have allowed them to travel on the road alone. They flew past us and we would have pulled the older boy up about it, but he was gone so fast that we were only able to look at each other in horror, and say: "Oh, my golly," and hope that they got home OK.

We looked back after them, holding our breath, as the bike and the two boys disappeared into the far distance. Then we carried on walking, discussing the awful types of parents that were bringing up children nowadays, but we got over it, and we resumed our walk. Only yards further on, we were waiting to cross at the pelican crossing. As it was a busy road, we had to wait for the lights to change. We perched at the edge of the kerb, waiting for our turn to cross the road. Finally the 'green man' pedestrian light appeared and Jo said, "Come on, let's go." But before we could even step off the pavement, a cyclist came from nowhere, right in front of us. He'd obviously run the red light. We turned our imminent step forward into a sway backwards. The cyclist was only inches away.

"Flippin' heck!" cried Jo, taking a proper leap back, "What *is* it with bikes today?"

I had no idea, but I let out the breath I'd been holding since the bike had skimmed my midriff, and we went on safely across the road. We carried on walking homewards. I must admit that by now I was looking around, waiting for the next bike, and wondering if this one was going hurtle onto the pavement to hit us, or if we were going to see someone killed under the wheels of a juggernaut. It made me feel very jumpy.

A little further on, at the next crossing, despite our caution, it happened again. Yet another cyclist shot the lights and whizzed past right in front of our noses. We both drew back and looked at one another in alarm.

"That's it!" I announced firmly, "It's a warning. We have to be very careful around pushbikes today."

As we carried on walking, I set my mind to wondering what

the warning was about. I envisaged one of our own kids falling off their bikes that evening as they played or that another bike would whizz by at any minute and knock us both flying. I got myself ready to lunge at any small child who passed by on a bike to stop them from being run over before our very eyes.

However, it seemed I was worrying about nothing because we got home without further mishap. We went indoors and grabbed a bite to eat before deciding to walk to the shopping precinct together for a spot of retail therapy. It was a pleasant sunny day, and we knew we just about had time to get there and back before the kids would be coming home from school. We'd almost forgotten about the bikes by then and we were strolling along nonchalantly, chatting about nothing in particular. But, halfway there, it all came together very suddenly. There was a public footpath emerging from the right, onto the pavement we were walking on, at right angles to it. Our minds barely had time to think...*bike! Look out! This is it!*

Like an avenging rocket, a teenager on a pushbike shot out from the footpath and hurtled across the pavement. He shot off into the road, and before we could even shout the abuse he surely deserved at him, he'd disappeared, peddling furiously, into the adjoining estate. We hadn't seen him approaching as he'd come full pelt at us, because a huge tall bush was in the way. He'd missed us by inches, but had totally ignored us. Jo and I had stopped dead in our tracks, safe behind the bush, and we looked at each other, eyes wide, thinking, *well that must have been it, we're safe now.*

I voiced our thoughts, "Thank goodness we had those warnings, because otherwise we might not have been quick enough to stop. Another near-miss – let's hope it's the last bike we see today!"

But, thank goodness our amazement at all the bike incidents made us pause for those vital few seconds, because coming along behind that cyclist, from behind this huge bush, at top speed, was a police transit van. There's no way we would have seen it coming in time. If we had carried on walking, without stopping to comment on our fourth bike-related incident of the day, the police van would have hit the pair of us for sure... We'd have been knocked over, and at the speed it was doing we would have been seriously injured or quite possibly killed. The police were obviously in hot pursuit after the bike-rider.

I'm still getting over it. The warnings weren't so much about bikes after all, but they were warnings nevertheless. If the other incidents hadn't taken place that day, we would have just carried on walking right into the path of the police van.

Jo refused to walk anywhere with me for a few weeks after that. She said she got goose-bumps every time she thought about it. I don't blame her, but I think we proved that day that *someone* up there is taking care of us. I always say that if you get shown more than three of anything, then it's a sure-fire signpost. I never expected four bikes to save my life though.

http://www.radicalpress.co.uk/Horoscopes.html

*

Gold Thread

Steve Sakellarios

In 1997, when I started my video production business, Gold Thread Video Productions, I decided that I also wanted to have a personal project going at the same time. I knew that if I waited until I had time, I'd never start it.

I had studied reincarnation as part of Eastern philosophy since a couple years after graduating high school, around 1973. But I knew very little about Western investigations. As I talked to people in casual conversation, I found that a surprising number of people had a personal experience related to reincarnation to tell, once they perceived that I wasn't going to make fun of them.

One morning, I woke with a start, and at that point I knew that the personal video project I wanted to do would be about reincarnation. It was as though the idea had sprung up overnight, or had been planted in my mind while I slept. But all I knew for sure was that the topic had been decided.

Almost this entire project was networked and built from nothing, and with essentially no funds, through the internet. But it wasn't all my doing. It seemed to have a life of its own.

One of the best examples was how Jeff Keene contacted me and became a part of the documentary. Jeff, an assistant fire chief, had just gotten access to the internet at his fire station. Searching on reincarnation, he got something like 30,000 hits, and noticed my website (I'm generally in the first fifty or so, but rarely toward the top).

He particularly noticed that I lived in the same city as his past-life personality, Atlanta, and he called me. I agreed that he should fly down (if I could get funding), and I began to conceive a plan to videotape a psychic past-life reading. This was quite a while before John Edward began Crossing Over. I obtained contacts for three local psychics through the Edgar Cayce Foundation. I was never able to make the arrangements with one of them, but when I called, I ended up speaking to a man named Steve at the front desk. At some point it came out in conversation that this man created electronic music, and we talked shop about video production and music. Finally, during the third or fourth conversation, he asked me what the purpose of the reading was. I explained to him that Mr Keene believed that he had been Confederate General John B. Gordon in a previous lifetime and I wanted to see if any information came out in the reading that would confirm it. (This wasn't very scientific of me in hindsight to reveal this information, but I never did use that particular psychic.) Steve exclaimed, "John B. Gordon? He was my great-

great uncle".

I arranged for Steve to meet Jeff when I flew Jeff down, and although I think Steve was skeptical at first, after a couple hours he was telling Jeff it had been an honor to meet him, so I presume he was convinced.

Now, this was just the first of a series of coincidences I experienced with Jeff. I decided to interview him right in front of General Gordon's gravesite (as you will see in the documentary), and I also arranged to videotape two psychic readings.

One was a numerological reading (for which I inadvertently distorted the audio) that mostly focused on Jeff's character in this lifetime, but the personality profile that emerged was highly consistent with what I later learned about the personality of General Gordon through studying his private papers.

The second reading was arranged hurriedly at the last minute, and was to be specifically a past-life reading. Neither psychic was given any advance information about Jeff, except his name and birth date. In the second reading (which is available for viewing in streaming video from the website at www.ial.goldthread.com) the psychic made references that could be construed as relevant to the past-life as Gordon, and the assessment of Jeff's character was very similar to the first reading.

However, the very first thing the psychic mentioned was very on-target for Jeff's most-recent past life. Jeff had briefly described his memories of this lifetime in a manuscript, written well before the videotaped psychic reading. As you compare the psychic reading and the manuscript, the parallels are quite striking, as you will be able to see for yourself on the website. Of course, I was hoping the psychic would say, "You were General Gordon in a past life," and nothing of the sort happened. I was disappointed, and yet I had the feeling there was some purpose behind it, that it wasn't so much a failure of the method, or an oversight, as something purposeful.

Sometime later, I met Jeff in Maryland at the Antietam

SUPER*naturally* True

Battlefield Park, to get shots of him at the scene where he had had his initial 'flashback' experience a year earlier.

I was combining this shoot with an interview with Carol Bowman, author of *Children's Past Lives*. I had been studying the phenomenon of young children talking about their previous lifetime up until about age seven, when typically they'd forget about it.

I had seen this happen once first-hand since I had been reading about it. I was videotaping a stage mind-reader (an entertainer), as part of my corporate video work. He was 'working the crowd' at a company picnic, and stopped to give a toy to a little girl who I would guess was about three years old, being pushed in a stroller by her mother. She had curly blond hair and large blue eyes. The mind-reader asked her, jokingly, "Are you married?" But he didn't stop to wait for an answer, he just began talking to the girl's mother. I, however, kept watching the girl for a response. I saw her get a very serious, far-away look in her eyes, and then it looked as though she was struggling inside herself for the answer. Finally, it seemed to me that she was trying to say something softly in the affirmative, but I couldn't hear her for the crowd noise. As we walked away, I asked the mind-reader, "What did the little girl say when you asked her if she was married?" He laughed and said, "What difference does it make?"

Now, I found myself in the museum of the Antietam Battlefield Park in Maryland. I was videotaping a sword handle on display, when I heard a young boy call out from about 15 feet behind me, "I know that man!"

I turned to see a boy about five years old come running up and stand next to me. He wasn't speaking about me. He was referring to a photograph of a Union soldier, John A. Tompkins, displayed behind the glass next to the sword handle I had been videotaping. He exclaimed again, "I know that man!" Quickly, I thought to myself, '*I need to ask open-ended questions, not leading ones*,' and I asked him, "Who is he?" The boy answered, "That's John." Which was correct, it was the name that was printed below the photograph. I asked, "What did he do?" and the boy answered, "He killed all the bad guys." Just then his parents came up, and I asked his mother if she thought he could have read the name. She said, "I don't know, he's just learning to read simple words." But the father was shaking his head, and said quietly, "He couldn't have read that."

So I felt it was an interesting coincidence that I was preparing to interview Carol Bowman, who studies this phenomenon, and an example of it had played out right before my eyes. But I certainly wasn't prepared for the next bit of synchronicity.

Jeff and I were standing in front of the motel where we were staying. Jeff had joined a Civil War enthusiasts' tour, and all the participants were booked at this same motel. Jeff and I were having a conversation about twenty feet from the entrance, in the circular driveway, and I was telling Jeff that one of my ancestors, by the name of Fidello Biddle, had actually been at the Antietam battle. As I said the name "Fidello Biddle," two men who were walking near the entrance – far enough away that I was amazed they could hear me at all in the open air – stopped and froze in their tracks. Then they came over to us. It was a man in his mid-thirties and an older man, who was his father as it turned out. One of them asked me point-blank, "Did you say, Fidello Biddle?" As it happened, Fidello was also their ancestor, and we were related. The older man turned out to be one of my mother's cousins, and they had some long phone conversations catching up subsequently.

These kinds of synchronistic experiences seem to occur more often than they normally would, where past-lives are involved. Recently, as I write this, I sold the first copy of *In Another Life*, by request to someone who contacted me through my website. It turned out that his brother produces documentaries on the Civil War, and had recently produced one on the Antietam Battle. When I mentioned this to Jeff, he knew of the production company and said he greatly admired their work. Jeff asked for the contact information, as he'd been trying without success to get on their website. To my knowledge the person buying the tape did not know that Jeff was in the video.

There have also been a great number of obstacles in producing this documentary, especially on such a meager budget. But often, in hindsight, it seems as though each obstacle acted to steer the project in a better direction, so that the final product you will see was shaped, over a five-year period, by my response to each obstacle. I hope the result conveys something of this tempering process to the viewer.

http://www.ial.goldthread.com

Chapter Eight

Supernatural Dreams

The common definition of dreams is that we symbolically sort through the events of the day while our minds are in a sleeping state. This makes sense most of the time, but there are two moments when we're in a different state – one just before sleeping and one just before waking. At these times our subconscious is available to us, and this can bring dreams that are inexplicable, dreams which can have far-reaching consequences. These are supernatural dreams.

A Mother's Love

Merryn Jose

"I'm very organized darling, my suitcases are packed, if there are any last minute items you'd like me to bring just leave a message. I'll be out a lot over the weekend seeing friends so don't worry if you can't reach me. I can't wait to see you both. I love you."

As I put the phone down, I was very happy that my mother Maureen, was coming from Hounslow in England to stay with me and my husband Julian, in our American home. She was a lot of fun and my friends were excited also as my mother was a professional clairvoyant would give some psychic readings for them during her stay. The last few days before her arrival were very busy, so on the Saturday morning, we decided to take a nap. It seemed that I had just laid my head on the pillow when I began to dream of my mother, who appeared to be in a very agitated state. I was talking to her on the telephone, and there was a lot of chaos and loud noise in the background. She seemed very frightened, telling me that she was going to die. Mum was disoriented, her words were slurred, and she was mumbling that she hadn't much time left.

I awoke in a panic and told Julian, "Something awful has happened to my mother!" I immediately telephoned her but there was no reply. Frustrated, I tried to contact a close friend who had a key to her home for emergencies, and he drove over to her flat.

When he called me from her home he said she wasn't there, but reported that the kettle was still plugged into the wall and the bed was unmade. She had obviously left in a great hurry. Eventually a neighbor told him that a woman had been taken away in an ambulance a day or so previously. He proceeded to call every hospital in the area and finally tracked her down. He raced over to the hospital and phoned us from her bedside. I tried to have a conversation with her on the phone but she made no sense at all. It was just like in the dream.

My husband and I took the first available flight to London and drove straight to the hospital.

Even though she recognized us, she was not really coherent and her voice kept trailing off in mid-sentence. I asked the night nurse why she had no Intravenous Drip in her arm and the nurse said she had been given the equivalent of two full IV bags and that was enough. She was also on antibiotics, and so the nurse said she should be fine.

We felt very uncomfortable with the prognosis. So first thing the next morning we contacted her private doctor who got the clearance to admit her to The Princess Grace Hospital in London. By then she was holding her head in her hands in great pain, saying that it felt as if it was about to burst.

Once she was admitted to the new hospital the doctors quickly discovered that she was severely dehydrated due to a chronic bladder infection. Her blood pressure was so high she was in danger of having a stroke at any moment. They said they would continue with the antibiotics and placed her on an IV drip for four consecutive days. After tests, she was given the correct blood pressure medication and the headaches ceased. It still took quite a while before she became truly coherent again.

Yes, her time had been running out, but because of our powerful bond, she was able to come to me in a dream to tell me she was in trouble, so that I could help her.

This is an extract from Merryn Jose's upcoming book.

Time and time again we see the deep connection between mother and daughter, which can never be broken. When a totally unexpected dream such as this occurs, and proves to contain true scenes, it can only be described as supernatural.

*

Eyes of an Angel

John Bankcroft

I had recurring dreams about eyes, up close, always the same eyes. It was very weird and after a while I started keeping notes. After a series of dreams I was able to draw the eyes. I knew their exact shade of blue, and the strange striations they contained, mostly black but with tiny amber lights in them. They were cat-like, while indisputably human, and the shape, size and lashes made them obviously female. The eyebrows were blond and fine and slightly arched. There was a pretty, tiny, black mole just below one delicate eyebrow.

I almost felt that I knew the owner without ever meeting her. I'd had a rocky history with relationships – married once and divorced, and several on-off attempts to find my soul mate after that.

I suppose I got a bit desperate to be honest. It's mostly women who worry about their biological clock, but I too felt time rushing by. I'd always wanted to have kids young. My Mum and Dad were older parents, they had careers first and then children. As a child I'd always felt that I missed out on the energy and enthusiasm they would have had for me if I was a baby when they were in their twenties or early thirties.

So, when my marriage broke up, although I knew deep down it would be for the best, I regretted losing the chance to start a family.

I didn't think I was too bad a catch; tall, dark, moderately good looking, and kind and considerate, so I wouldn't make a bad Dad or husband.

I came close two years ago, when I met a woman who seemed perfect, and miraculously she seemed to feel the same way about me, but, as I discovered during a deep conversation, she didn't want to have children, ever. It wouldn't have been fair to either of us, so we split. I was back to being single and there followed a series of unfortunate and mistaken attempts at finding that elusive partner. Relationships became stressful, and I lost the ability to have fun with someone, which I guess made things worse.

Then the dreams about the eyes started. After some time I took comfort in the dreams, but it was frustrating never to see the woman's face. I wanted to believe that the dreams meant something, were trying to tell there *was* someone out there for me. But in honesty I felt it was more likely they were just a creation of wishful thinking.

I stopped looking for partners, and almost became a bit of a recluse. Then one day, it happened. I'd been dragged to a party held by some friends. I was bored, not wanting to be there among all those happy couples.

I'd said no when I was invited, but fate had other ideas. The night before the party I had another dream about the eyes, her eyes, and in the dream I could hear music and laughter, and I thought, mmm…maybe I was meant to go to the party. So I went.

When I got there I was full of expectation, thinking any minute I'll see *her*. But of course it didn't work that way. At midnight I decided to call it a day, go home to my lonely bed. I called a taxi because I'd had a few drinks. When it arrived I dropped into the back seat and I was pretty amazed to see from the back of the driver's head that she was a woman – or a guy with long, curly, blond hair. Unusual to have a female driver, I thought, at this time of night, and not particularly safe for her. To put her at ease, I tried to sound really friendly and nice. "Evening. Can you take me to Gulliver Terrace please?"

She glanced up at the rear view mirror, and her eyes met mine. It was *those eyes!* My heart started beating like a drum. It was her! The same colors, the same eyebrows, and the same little mole.

"Sure," she answered, taking her gaze from the mirror.

I didn't know what to do. I couldn't tell her the truth, could I? It would sound like the world's worst chat up line! I decided to play it cool. I made a note of the taxi company and when I got out at home, I only met her eyes for a few seconds as I paid her.

"Be safe," was all I could manage as she pulled away.

I used that same taxi company every night for a week, and three times I was lucky. I gradually found out with gentle questions that she was the mother of a little girl, aged one. Her husband turned out to be violent, and they'd divorced before the baby was born. He'd then skipped town, so she was doing the late night shifts to earn enough to put a deposit on a home for her and her daughter, who slept every night at her mum's.

Well, you can guess, a year later we were married. Not only did my dreams foretell my soul mate's arrival, but I even got a ready-made daughter, the sweetest child ever.

Carrie and I and little Cara live together in my house, and we are blissfully happy. The icing on the cake is that Carrie is pregnant with our child as I write. Did I ever tell her about the dream? Yes, I thought I should – no secrets. She thought it was wonderful, romantic and confirmed what she already knew, that we are soul mates, and nobody and nothing can keep soul mates apart for long!

Many of us daydream of perfect love, but this was pure premonition. These dreams show a deep karmic connection between this man and his future wife. They most likely spent many past lives together, and the dream came from their connection on a soul level.

*

Disconnecting

Ann Mullen

One Sunday morning, I awoke early with heaviness in my heart. I felt alone, that separate feeling that happens when someone very much loved dies. My first reaction was to reach across the bed to make sure my husband was breathing, the feeling was that strong. Randall was fine, and I tried to push the darkness out of my mind.

"Hey, Babe. You awake?" I asked.

"Yeah. You ready for a cup of coffee? I'm about to make that first run."

"Sure, bring me a cup."

I sat up in bed, and as Randall crawled back in, we talked for a minute before turning on the television. On Sunday mornings, we often watch a Joel Osteen presentation to get our weekly dose of inspiration. His speech was the usual applied Christianity in that he reminded us that the only guarantee for a happy life is to help others. I had a difficult time focussing on his words. The heaviness in my heart was almost overwhelming. After the service was over, I mentioned my sadness to Randall.

"I don't know why, but I'm really teary-eyed today."

"Is it something I've said or done?" he joked.

I smiled. "No! I don't know why. I just feel so sad."

We talked about other things, including the baby shower we were scheduled to attend later in the day.

"You know, Randall, I would really like to stay home today. I'm in a dark place. Maybe I should just be by myself. Why don't you and Peggy, go?" (Peggy is Randall's sister).

"Ann. I really want you to go with us. Tell me what's wrong."

He looked disappointed, and I didn't really know what was wrong. I couldn't put my finger on it, so I agreed to go to the get-together.

Maybe it will be good for me to get out of the house. I have no reason to be sad.

With those thoughts, I put on my happy face for the day. I made small talk. We went out to an early dinner with a couple of friends from the party. I did everything I knew to get past the ominous feeling that seemed to hang heavy on my mind. When we got home, I spent a couple of hours writing. I can usually get lost in writing and find a new outlook at the end of the road, but not this time. Eventually, I gave up and went to bed. Mondays are not my favorite days, but as I got dressed for work, I had to admit my heart was lighter. I met a co-worker for coffee and chatter, and by nine o'clock, I decided life was good again. Around ten-thirty, my daughter, Mary, who is also my business partner, and I were talking about work. In the middle of our conversation, she stopped suddenly.

"Oh, Mom, I've got to tell you something!"

"What?"

"I had a dream about Daddy last night. It wasn't sad or anything, but I feel like I need to tell you about it."

"Okay."

So far, the conversation was not unusual. Mary has dreamt many times about her Dad, Ronnie, since his death in January, 2003. She loves to tell me about her dreams, and we both enjoy sharing them. Even though I'd married Randall in 2006, and was very happy with him, I would always miss Ronnie.

"This dream was different than all the others. You know how Daddy always looks like he's about forty-five in my dreams, dark hair, and slimmer, like when I was a teenager?"

I nodded and she continued to relate her experience.

"Well, in this dream, he looked exactly like he looked the last time I saw him, on that Monday night right before he left the office, when he said, '*See you tomorrow, Honey girl.*' I noticed the way he looked, right off. And it didn't feel like you were there."

Now I was puzzled. "What do you mean? Of course, I wasn't there. I'm here!" We both laughed, and she continued.

"That's not what I mean. I don't know if I can even explain what I mean except to say it felt like you and Daddy weren't together. So I asked him about it. I asked him if y'all were together, and he said 'No'. Then, I asked him why did y'all get a divorce, and, Mom, these were his exact words:"

'*Honeygirl, we didn't get a divorce. We just aren't together any more.*'

"When I said to him that I thought everything was perfect with you guys, he laughed, and he sounded just like he always did when he laughed. You know, like he was in on the joke. Anyway, he said yes, it was a good time. He said y'all were soul mates, and Mom, this is the really weird part, a guy named Billy Nava appeared next to him."

I had not heard the name before, so I asked Mary about it. "Who's Billy Nava?"

"Billy Nava was the dad of one of the baseball boys."

My son-in-law coaches a high school baseball team, and one of the players had recently lost his father, Billy Nava, to cancer. I could not fathom how my late husband would have known him on this side, much less the other side, but I encouraged Mary to finish her story.

"So, what happened next?"

"Well, Billy was standing there next to Dad. Mom, I'm not kidding you, it was so real I felt as if I could reach out and touch them! Daddy looked directly at me, in my eyes, and said: *'Billy, here, told me I need to move on now. I've got stuff to learn and I should go on down the road. I've decided to do that. Your mama's okay.'*

"It felt so real. I thought it was really happening until I woke up!"

Then, I told her about my Sunday and that distinct feeling of losing a connection.

"Your dad never could sneak off, could he? He always ended up telling me exactly where he was going – even when he didn't plan to."

We both laughed because life is good, and it never ends.

We discovered that Billy Nava was a Teamster truck driver, as was my late husband. Perhaps they ran into each other somewhere during his lifetime, or maybe those union guys are in a special place!

My daughter called Billy Nava's widow to see if there was some connection which we were unaware of between her late husband and mine. Turns out Billy's father-in-law (and her dad) worked several years with my late husband at Red Ball Motor Freight. This connection made the dream and message all the more believable.

Because what one believes becomes the truth for them, those of us who believe in a soul's ability to reach through the invisible curtain are touched more often than those who don't. While the space between our souls may seem more distant, we remain connected forever.

www.randall-m.com

Ronnie is the most thoughtful man, even after death. He knew that there was a part of Ann that still needed to let go of the past, in order to fulfill her true potential in the future. He used his strong connection to his daughter to relay the message, to make absolutely sure that Ann took it seriously.

Chapter Nine

Unusual Manifestations

God works in mysterious ways, and so do spirits. When someone has first died, apparently they can be confused and not really know the ropes to send a message to their loved ones that they're safe. They can end up using all kinds of strange ways to get through; animals, objects, even modern technology.

*

Text Messages from Spirit

Jeane Dutton-Hill

My friend Jill Hocking was born on October 5th 1979 and passed away on May 9th 2004. So she was only 24 when she died after a long battle with cystic fibrosis. She was a brave and beautiful inspiration to us all.

Jill achieved so much during her short life; she was an amazing artist; she obtained a degree, she won an award from the Cystic Fibrosis Trust, and she brought so much fun and laughter into the lives of everyone who knew her. We still miss her terribly. Jill lived most of her life in Marlow, Buckinghamshire; she did well at school and was a popular pupil. She loved gymnastics and art. After leaving school she moved to Nottingham to enroll at Nottingham University to study art. She moved back down to Staines two years ago to be nearer to the Brompton Hospital in Kensington, where she spent much of her later life.

Despite her illness she never complained and she was loved by all the hospital staff. She decorated her hospital room with fairy lights and anything pink and fluffy. Pink and fluffy summed Jill up, it was a color she wore often and at times even her hair was pink! She had a great sense of decoration and style and would come up with amazing ideas for her artwork. One of her projects involved making a quilt out of cabbage leaves and it was displayed on a bed complete with Jill sleeping in it! She was ill for months afterwards because the decaying leaves affected her lungs but she didn't mind suffering for her art one bit. To her the rotting leaves represented her lungs. She hated mushrooms too and would make sculptures of them with cocktail sticks sticking in them so they "hurt" – again like her lungs, grey and decaying.

In February 2004 Jill underwent a double lung transplant. We hoped it would lead to a better quality of life for her and our thoughts and prayers were with the family who lost a child in order to give Jill the gift of life. Sadly it wasn't meant to be; initially Jill appeared to be doing well but after three months she developed an infection in her heart, lungs and brain. She underwent heart surgery and basically never fully regained consciousness. The doctors discovered that her vital organs were shutting down. There was nothing more they could do. Only the life support machine was keeping her alive. Her family and I were with her at the end holding her hands and telling her how much we loved her. I said it was all right for her to leave us and go to her grandmother, Auntie Mary and Uncle Joe, who would look after her and show her what to do. Her life support machine was switched off and she slipped away peacefully, free of pain and suffering at last.

We try to remember the good times, like the day I was pushing her over the bridge in Staines, when she had to use a wheel chair. Gathering speed I asked her where the brake was. She replied there wasn't one! Picture if you will Jill gripping the arms and me hanging on to the handles for dear life at 60mph whilst approaching a dual carriageway! Then there was the time in hospital where we swapped places and I nearly got wheeled off to x-ray. We were terrible! There was also the small incident of my American crocodile shoes being used to grow bulbs in. I didn't know anything about it until I saw her photographs from her art exhibition at college!

A few months ago I sat in her bedroom holding the container of her ashes and talking to her as I often did. I laughed as I was relaying something funny and a flower decoration fell off her bedroom wall. That was when I knew she could still hear me!

I was Jill's godmother, she always called me her 'fairy godmother'. It was extremely hard to carry on without her. The grief was unbearable at times, particularly Christmas and her birthday. Even now I still pick up anything pink and fluffy when I'm out shopping thinking Jill would love this and then turning towards the cash desk, I remember, she's gone.

I would always consult her about what I should wear if I was going somewhere special and ask her advice about things in general. She was wise beyond her years and used to joke about the way I seemed to lurch from one disaster to the next and said I needed 'someone to look after me'.

Six months after she died I met up with an old friend I hadn't seen for years in rather bizarre circumstances and we started seeing each other. He totally understands my need to talk about Jill and have what he refers to as my 'Jill moments', where I recall something amusing or I'm just thinking about her a lot. We are now engaged. He's the love of my life and takes care of me. I know it's all down to Jill – making sure someone is looking after me!

I saved two of Jill's last text messages on my phone. One was about Concorde. Jill adored the aircraft, and would go and watch it take off or land at Heathrow airport, whenever she was well enough. These messages were precious to me, a connection, and a way to make me feel that she was still with me. One day, in sheer desperation of finding a way to reach her, I asked for a sign she was OK. Hours later my mobile phone beeped, twice – two messages had come through. They were the same messages I had saved, the last messages from Jill. They were both marked as 'sender unknown', where it should have given the number. It was her way of telling me she was up flying up there with Concorde and was doing fine!

I set up a memorial website in her name to raise money for the Cystic Fibrosis Trust and awareness about this terrible life threatening disease. Cystic Fibrosis is the UK's most common life-threatening, inherited disease. Symptoms include poor weight gain and repeated chest infections. It is a genetic disease that affects a number of organs in the body, especially the lungs and pancreas by clogging them with thick sticky mucus. At present there is no cure for Cystic Fibrosis, but the faulty gene has been identified and doctors and scientists are working to find ways of repairing or replacing it.

www.homestead.com/askjeane

Using modern technology helped Jill get a message through to her friend. Some spirits seem to be able to use all manner of things. I don't want to leave this plane yet, but I must say I'm intrigued to find out how all this works!

*

Numbers

Sandra King

My friend Matt had been dead for almost a year and it was the day after his birthday. I had come in from work and no one else was there. When I walked in I remember thinking the electricity was off because the air was so still and static. Suddenly the stereo turned on and instead of being static sounding, it was this crackling sound. Right then a loud and clear voice said, "It's Matt," and the stereo turned off. My heart just pounded and I knew it was real, it was very exhilarating.

The second time is kind of a funny thing. When my friend was alive he used to come over to my ex boyfriend's house and adjust the time on this large clock over the fireplace. The clock had no batteries and he'd always move the time to 4:20 (he thought it was funny). Well long after me and that guy broke up and my friend had died, I was sitting in a new house looking at this little clock above the fireplace that didn't have batteries. The date was April 20th and I was thinking about how Matt used to change the clock. Just then the hands on this clock started spinning around and stopped at 4:20. *No way* was it a coincidence, no way at all. It didn't even have batteries in it. So, both clocks were above the fireplace and neither had batteries and it moved to 4:20 on the date of 20th of the 4th.

I love spirits with a sense of humor, and that applies to both the last stories!

*

Spoons

Ann Mullen

On January 4, 2003, my husband and I were returning from a couple of days of play. It was late and dark and we were talking non-stop as we always did even when we drove home. The subject of crossing over and death came up. I had lost five relatives in the past year and we talked about Where they might be; what they might be; how they might be? Death conversations were never macabre with us. They always seemed natural and open and inquisitive. This night's exchange of ideas seemed a little more serious, but not scarily serious, just interestingly serious.

Ron and I had been married forty years, less about three weeks and, at some point in the discussion, we made a pact that the one of us who found ourselves first on the other side would attempt to contact the one left behind, to give a small concrete sign that life does indeed go on.

That brief exchange of ideas and promises between two healthy adults with plans to live many, many more years resurfaced within a fortnight and with surprising clarity. We traveled a lot and wherever we went, we collected spoons. Over the last several years, we had taken several trips one month to three months long, and for our last year together we rolled along in an Alfa Gold Fifth Wheel. We worked as camp hosts, we hiked, birded, built trails, went sightseeing, hit the casinos, and we collected spoons. Ronnie died nine days before we were to leave on a thirty day trip to Australia and New Zealand to celebrate our fortieth wedding anniversary. Anticipating the spoons we would collect had made the planning of it more intriguing.

Our collection of spoons began in 1977 in Denver, Colorado, the first of many vacations we would share with Bets, my mother in law. She bought a spoon rack for me to display spoons commemorating the sites we saw. Spoons from every National Monument, National Park, restored fort, ghost town, every place we visited, graced that first rack and I guess the collecting of spoons transfused our blood, Ronnie's even more so than mine. Over the years, he selected and purchased eight more spoon racks with capacities varying from twelve to forty-eight spoons each, and displayed them on our living room walls. Everywhere we went, we searched for the perfect spoon to perpetuate that specific spot in our minds.

The one rule was: never display any spoon unless we had visited the place, a rule set aside when Jessie, our granddaughter, brought us three from her European trip. Still, those spoons hung separately on a row segregated from the ones saluting our incredible times together.

During the summer of 2002, Ron and I talked a lot about our spoons as we wandered from place to place across the Midwest from Mall of the Americas to Glacier National Park and, at every stop, we bought another one, twenty-one in all – the most we had ever collected in one year. We re-lived in our conversations those times past already memorialized by spoons on the racks at home. We returned home in November to place our new spoons on those racks and visualized the ones to come next year. Reservations were made at two of Australia's National Parks, there would be spoons from there. The casino in Melbourne where we would spend our anniversary night would offer a special spoon. Jessie told the innkeeper at the Tasmania bed and breakfast of our hobby and he promised to have one ready. And she even convinced the horse ranch where she worked to have something to add to our collection.

About 5:30 in the afternoon of January 6, 2003, Ron and I were walking our dog. We'd had a busy day, me packing for Australia and Ron running errands for the office. Ron was more tired than usual, yet we both laughed when he said, "Those girls at the office don't know I'm retired, or they just don't care!" About half way into our mile and a half loop walk, he became dizzy and light-headed and sat down to rest a minute. I told him I would drive over to pick him up after I finished the walk and Niki and I continued down the trail. From about 250 yards away I saw he had crossed the creek and was walking toward the locked car. *Why?* I thought. *I had the keys. Why didn't he wait for me?* When I looked over again, he was lying on the ground. I raced toward him, thinking he must have tripped or perhaps he had lost his balance and may have hurt a knee, or twisted an ankle.

A couple reached him first. He was lucid, not in any pain. I asked him and he said, "No, just very weak and lightheaded." I backed the car and the couple helped him in. He thanked them and was dead less than a full minute later. He never struggled, gasped for breath or expressed any indication of pain. He simply stopped breathing. He was pronounced dead on arrival at the hospital. Based on what had happened, doctors speculated electrical imbalance, cardiovascular disease or a stroke, and in the end, the death certificate listed 'heart attack'.

No one asked to perform an autopsy, it didn't seem necessary. Certainly not to me. He was gone and the why or how didn't really matter. I signed a form to donate his organs as we had agreed long ago and knew he would be pleased to know someone would see with his corneas, maybe the only usable donation. I was lost in a fog of disbelief, as were our kids, our grandchildren and all of the people who loved him. Ronnie and I enjoyed the being together part of being married and I could not get my mind around the thought of not having Ronnie next to me. Once, just a few months before, in Deadwood, South Dakota, Ron and I became separated in one of the casinos. Thinking I had left the building, he went down the street and, when I realized he was gone, I panicked, consumed by an unreasonable fear of losing him. As I dashed from building to building in search of him, while he searched for me. When we saw each other, I burst into tears and even though I felt foolish, I couldn't stop the tears of relief. He understood and held me for a minute.

Maybe that was a precursor of things to come. The same horror and terror multiplied a thousand, a million times devoured my spirit that Monday afternoon and grew to a massive hole in my heart by five days later, Saturday morning, the day of the memorial service.

Our kids, my brother John, my niece Peggy, my sister-in-law Becky, and a couple of friends, arrived early that morning for coffee and to prepare for our formal good-byes. While the others sat in the living room, John and I sat at the kitchen table talking, reminiscing about how Ronnie had added so much to both of our lives. John, who was to do the eulogy, made notes as he put together his farewell tribute. Then the sound of something hitting the floor in the living room pierced the heavy air that surrounded us. A spoon had fallen from the top rack.

In the 25 years that those racks hung on that wall, never had a spoon fallen. Most of them could only be removed when turned at certain angle. Peg called out, "Aunt Olevia, a spoon fell." Olevia was my name as a youth and still is as far as my family was concerned. It was Ronnie who started calling me Ann, which was my other birth name.

Chill bumps covered my arms as I reached to pick up the fallen spoon. It was from Tombstone, Arizona, a place we had visited so long ago. Without a voice, Ronnie spoke to me and I heard him as clearly as if he sat across the room. "Ann, I've crossed. The tombstone of my life has been set. You will go on and we will still travel together."

Becky said, "Look. The spoon next to the one that fell is moving."

Indeed it was swinging back and forth and I got a chair to climb up to look at it. Australia? How could that be? We were never in Australia. Australia was just a place we had planned to visit together.

I don't know the source of the Australia spoon and in a way it doesn't matter how it found a place in our spoon collection. Ronnie spoke to me, to all of us, as we sat discussing his life. He let me know I was not alone, and that he would stand beside me even as I stood at his tombstone, and he would continue to travel with me.

I experienced a peace unknown that week and peace remains with me. It got me through that day and every day since. There have been dozens of other reminders of Ronnie's continued presence in my life, but none clearer or more opportune than the falling of the spoon.

www.randall-m.com

Ronnie actually created a spoon, which I've never heard of before. Apports are objects that manifest suddenly from the spirit world, normally dropping onto the floor, but it's new to me that a spirit could carefully place an object on a hook. What a clever way to send a message

*

The Spirit of Jesus Set Me Free

Alice Jean

I had a very powerful spiritual experience when I was 30 years old. I turned seventy years old this March, and if I just recall this experience it's like it was yesterday.

To tell this story I have to go back even further to the age of eighteen.

I ran away from home to a big city when I was eighteen, and learned that it was a very frightening, mean place for a young girl. I got little jobs as a waitress and sometimes had no place to live. I even slept in doorways and the park. I was raped several times in that city.

One time, a guy took me to an apartment telling me he had to see his mother. No mother there, just five more guys. Somehow I snuck out of there, quietly ran down three flights of stairs, and onto the street where I continued to run in fear. My heart was pounding through my chest as I ran and ran around two corners before I realized I was not being followed. I heard a voice in my head very calmly say, "It's all right, it's all right. You only have until you're around thirty."

"What does that mean?" I said out loud. Probably means I'll die at thirty.

Now I'll fast-forward to my 30th birthday. I had never remembered that incident from years ago until I was writing a letter to my younger brother to tell him what it felt like to be thirty. In those days, we talked about being 'over the hill' at thirty. Old! I had written a paragraph of my letter, and it all came back in a flash. Oh God what have I done? I was told I only had until I was 30, and then I brought four children into this world, four children who will soon lose their mother.

I was beside myself with grief. I became very depressed. Every day I expected to just drop dead. Or the husband who was physically and emotionally abusive would maybe hit me a little too hard next time and kill me. Day after day I became more and more depressed over this and at one time, on Mother's Day, I even thought of counting up all the pills in the house and doing myself in. That thought didn't last long as soon as I wondered what then would happen to my little children. But I still thought I was going to die, somehow.

This violent man I was married to worked night-shift. One night not long after I had gotten into bed, saying my prayers, I began to cry. I was calling on Jesus to help me and forgive me for all the bad things I had done in my life. I was reviewing my whole life and taking the blame for everything that had ever happened to me, including the rapes. Tears were running down the sides of my face into my ears as I was weeping.

In this dark room, I began to realize that there was a golden light glow filling the air. Things were kind of blurred through my tears, but I could see a figure and just knew it was the one I was calling. Jesus stretched his arms out to me from the ceiling and I raised my arms up and flew into his arms. It was a very sensual experience as I felt his garments wrap around me and his hair touching my face which had been soaked in tears. We spun around and around and I have never felt as loved, before or since.

He then whispered in my ear, "There is NOTHING to forgive." Those words, I think, put me in ecstasy. Soon, everything was fading and I was in my bed, hands clasped in prayer and my face was dry. I have no idea how long this lasted. Maybe a split second...or hours? I woke up the next morning a different person.

Everyone noticed it just looking at my face. I had women friends ask me if I had changed my hair, or make-up, or what was it? I was no longer afraid of anything! I began to make my plans for taking my children and leaving that place and the way of living like a prisoner in terror.

Some while after the divorce, I met a man through mutual friends, who has been, and still is the love of my life. He pointed out that in photographs of before and after that wonderful night, I looked ten years younger after, and had a different 'look'. I thank God every day for my life!

In this case, a physical embrace was used to make the point very clear and very real. This episode completely changed Alice's life.

*

Dad Found a Way

Dana Forest

My Dad, David, was a lovely bloke, everybody liked him and he would always stop to chat to people. He was a happy go lucky chap and was always whistling.

He worked all his life, doing various jobs, right up until he died at age 74. He was a very kind hearted man with a soft spot for animals, and was not able to stand to see an animal ill treated. He would do anything to help anyone out, especially his children, and he was a great Dad. Even my Mum, Lorraine, says she couldn't fault him as a father, and that he even helped change nappies. They had three children, my elder sister and brother, Doreen and Darren, and me, Dana, the youngest.

Even when we were adults he always helped us out. I remember one night when I was about eighteen years old I was not able to get a taxi home. I rang Dad at around 3am and he came and picked me and my friend up without a moan. He was such a good Dad and I'll never forget everything he did for me.

Dad was seventy-four when he died, but he'd never forgive me if I didn't tell you that although he was twenty years older than my Mum, he looked much younger than his real age, by at least ten years, and people were shocked at how old he really was.

What happened to Dad was a tragedy that none of us saw coming.

He and my brother Darren, worked at the same air conditioning company. Darren found out that Dad had been getting a little over friendly with a young lady at work. He would buy her cigarettes and sandwiches and give her money. Dad was working as a warehouse-man and didn't earn much money, so he would tell my Mum that he had lost the odd tenner here and there, and Mum was already becoming a bit suspicious. One lunch-time my brother saw my Dad giving his friend her lunch and buying her some cigarettes, and told Dad if he didn't stop it he'd tell my Mum. Bear in mind that she was twenty-one and my dad was seventy-four! This went on for a while and Darren was getting angry about it. Dad said if Darren told Mum he would only cause trouble. Sometimes Dad and Darren both went home for lunch, and on this particular day Darren said he had had enough and was telling Mum, and he did. Understandably, she hit the roof.

Meanwhile Dad came to my house and he was acting very odd. In five years he had never come to my house, because he didn't get on with my partner, so I knew something was going on. We chatted for a while, and it was all at bit strange. Then he said he was leaving and he'd be in touch. I said goodbye and gave him a hug and a kiss and told him I loved him.

I wanted to stop him, but I was still in my night clothes, so I let him drive away. As I waved to him I just knew I'd never see him again.

I immediately got a phone call from Mum saying she had noticed a lot of tablets had gone missing, and we both panicked. I picked my Mum up and we went to look for him.

We searched for about 45 minutes at his work place, but with no luck, so nervously we went home. When we got home my Mum and I found Dad upstairs in the spare bedroom. He had taken an overdose, and was not breathing. Knowing some CPR, I tried desperately to save him, and I did get his pulse going, but we were told later that we were about five minutes too late to save him.

So basically Dad killed himself in his lunch break over something so ridiculous it's unbelievable. Dad knew Mum would be fuming and thought she would throw him out, and he loved my Mum and his two dogs so much that he couldn't bear to live without them. He was just not the sort of person to kill himself, and no-one could believe what he'd done. Even now people still comment on it.

He was probably just being kind to the girl, because that's what he was, kind and thoughtful, which makes it even worse. Dad was a strict non-believer, and always said, "When you're dead that's it!" My Mum and brother half-believed but were open minded, but Mum is a definite believer now because something very strange happened. I'm a total believer and always have been. As a young child I always seemed to experience unexplainable things!

When it came time to arrange the funeral, we were all talking about how we had never got to say goodbye to Dad. It seemed very unfair of such a good Dad, to leave us so suddenly, with no warning. Of course he'd obviously come to see me to say goodbye, but I hadn't known it, and the rest of the family, especially Darren, felt abandoned.

The Vicar came to our house one Sunday lunch-time, to discuss arrangements, and the things that would be said at his funeral.

We were all still in shock and so sad, but we tried to talk to the Vicar as best as we could. When he asked us what sort of things my Dad liked to do, we were all a bit stuck. Dad had a full life, but he worked a lot and didn't have any particular interests. By a bizarre coincidence we all said at the same time, "He loved to feed the birds!"

Well it *would* have been just a coincidence, but on the word 'birds' we heard this loud flapping, scraping sound. We ignored it for as long as possible, but it got louder and scratchier, until the Vicar had to say something. We were baffled as to what it was, but we eventually came to the conclusion a bird had fallen down the chimney and was trapped behind the fireplace. The Vicar was a bit shocked, but not as shocked as us because my parents had lived in that house for 36 years, and it had never happened before. As far as my Mum knew there was a net cover over the chimney pot hole.

My brother and I spent the next few hours trying to remove a very complex gas fire, piece by piece. As it was a Sunday, no gas man wanted to come out, as it wasn't an emergency, and it would have cost a fortune anyway. Four hours later we eventually got to the back of the fire, and it was just a spooky dark hole with no bird in sight. We were both a bit annoyed, but I said I'd put a glove on and shove my hand up. I felt around but couldn't feel anything at all, and I pulled my hand out in disgust, thinking what a waste of time that had all been. Then I nearly had a heart attack! Sitting quietly on my hand was a sooty looking starling. It wasn't flapping about like they usually do, but just sat there looking at me. Then it casually flew onto a nest of tables that my Dad used to always have his cup of tea on. It then flew onto the back of my Dad's armchair, and sat there for a while, not seeming the slightest bit scared or bothered. I'm not sure who suggested that this was my Dad come back to see us, but we all spoke to the bird as if it was him. It was a very, very surreal moment, and one I'll never forget.

I opened the window to let the bird out, but it just hopped onto the window sill. It could have easily flown out, but it turned around and just looked straight at us for a moment while we stood there like three statues!

By now it was early evening and the sun was bright orange and quite low. This strange little starling opened its wings and seemed to head straight for the sun. We watched it for as long as we could until it just disappeared into the sun's orange glow, and our eyes hurt from the brightness.

We were amazed, and were all in tears. It still brings a tear to my eye now just thinking about it. We all felt that my Dad had been with us that afternoon, and it was his only way of saying goodbye. While I was writing this I swear I felt him over my shoulder.

Some people may think we're crazy but nothing will ever take that memory away from me. I know what happened that day may be hard for some people to believe, but there is no doubt in my mind whatsoever. This happened before his funeral and I also saw and spoke to him a few times. When someone kills themself, the family are left with a lot of questions. Dad answered most of mine, and I know he regrets what he did. He really did have a reason to come back and say goodbye to us.

My Mum confirmed that we just knew the bird was Dad. She sometimes tells the story and she always says, "He was a bird." What I say is, "What happened to white doves eh, trust my dad to pick a scraggy old starling instead!"

I think this particular Dad knew that his family wasn't best pleased with him for leaving the way he did, without a goodbye and without taking the blame. I think he thought that by using a bird he would get them to remember the good times, the funny times, and not dwell so much on the way of his passing.

Chapter Ten

Near Death Experiences

So what of those of us who have peeped through the veil between this physical life and that of spirits? People who have come back to tell the tale? These stories that follow will amaze you. When I read some of them I thought it might almost be worth being taken to the brink of death in order to see what these people saw there.

A Good Day to Die?

John Ingram

I remember hearing a Native American song that included the words 'a good day to die' and I think I must have had a premonition that day because these words popped into my head as I got out of bed. But they had a question mark at the end of them, rather than as if they were just stating a fact.

I'm a diabetic, and that means I live constantly on the edge, so the words didn't scare me like they might have done otherwise.

It started off as a great day anyway, the sun was shining, the surf was up, and everything was right with the world, so I soon forgot the words I'd woken up with, and got on with living as I'd learned to. Sometimes that 'living' meant I indulged in a bit more of life's culinary treats that was good for me, but I was still not too fat to surf, so that was OK! I'd gotten away with playing 'chicken' with my blood sugar for this long! So, one minute I was riding the waves, so happy, so full of life, and then the next thing I knew I was falling onto the sand, weak, fluid legs, unable to hold me up. I was disorientated, dizzy and fading fast.

I think it took some while for anyone to notice that I wasn't just sun-bathing, but eventually I sensed people gathered round me. I tried to speak, tried to tell them what I needed, but I couldn't form any words. Their faces spun around me and then it all went dark, just as my fuzzy hearing heard the sirens.

I came round, I don't know how much later because something was tapping the back of my head. Eventually, annoyed, I reached up to feel what it was and realized it was something hard and unyielding, but the thing that made me open my eyes was that I realized I was bumping into it, upwards, rather than the other way round. Then I wished I still had my eyes closed, because I was floating up by the ceiling, and that was what I was bumping, as I bobbed gently up and down against it.

I blinked rapidly and the scene below me which was of a body on a trolley, covered with a sheet, had vanished. Instead the ceiling had melted away, because I was outside, under the stars and I was sailing up away from the hospital roof.

I felt sick and scared as the land below me swung away and I was turned over in mid-flight. I was now facing a bright white light that opened into a tunnel. It was brightly lit inside and before I could blink, I was rushing along inside it. Ahead of me I could make out shadowy figures, their shapes bleached out by the bright light. They slowly came into focus. One of them was light like a stereotypical angel, wings and everything, but I didn't have eyes for him. Beside him was my Mom, and my eyes filled with tears as she smiled lovingly at me and opened her arms. We hugged and I hadn't felt so happy for years, not really since she'd died. All I wanted right then was to stay there with her, but she gently pushed me back so that I could see her face.

"Baby boy," she said, "Go back. Make me proud. You'll be with me soon enough."

She gave me a little shove and I started falling back down the tunnel. I sobbed like a baby as I saw my Mom's figure dwindle away, and then there was an explosion, a bang, behind me. I shut my eyes and just like that I was back in my body.

I could feel something on my eyes, and I sensed it was a sheet. They thought I was dead! I didn't know what to do.

Those words from my Mom had changed me. I realized that I had been wasting my life, not living it. I really, really, wanted a chance to do what she'd said. I was galvanized and wanting to prove to her that I could be the son she wanted me to be, in her memory. But there was a problem. They thought I was dead, and I was terrified. Then I heard a sound that scared me even more. It was my sister Megan's voice, and she was crying. Someone was bringing her along to identify my body. Once that was done I assumed I'd be put 'on ice' and that would really be the end.

My sister and the attendant reached my trolley and the sheet was rolled back. My eyes were shut as if glued and no part of my body would move. My sister spoke my name and touched my hand. I tried to move it, to squeeze her fingers, but I couldn't do it. The sheet fell back onto my hand. I cried out to my Mom in my head, asking her to help me. She'd wanted me to go back and I was trying, so hard. Suddenly, my lips pursed together and my cheeks puffed out, filled with air. I blew, as hard as I could, and I felt the sheet flutter. Thank God Megan saw it move and she screamed. The next half an hour was a flurry of activity as the doctors did their work and brought me the rest of the way back. Thank you Mom. I will make you proud...

I wonder what strings John's Mum pulled to give her son this talking to and another chance to live the rest of his life?

*

The Angry Angel That Brought Me Back

Steve Patchelli

I'm Italian by birth, fiery by nature. I'm not in the least like someone who'd see an angel. I drink a lot, drive fast, play hard...well at least I used to. Not any more though. One night, five years ago I was driving, fast as usual, along the freeway. Suddenly red lights flashed ahead of me, a truck braking. As I got closer, I didn't brake. I was just going to sail past him. The only thoughts in my head were, no way *I'm gonna get held up by that slowpoke!* What I didn't know that the carriageway was closed off ahead, because I was driving so close to the back of the truck, I didn't see the signs. I swept into the fast lane, pulling around the truck. Next thing I knew, a dimly-lit construction machine loomed in my headlights. It was him or the truck. In a split second I knew I'd have a better chance against the truck – he had a flat end, and the machinery had a big bucket on my side. I could hear my brakes squealing and I knew I had no chance. Bang! I hit him.

From then on, all I knew for some time was blackness, then my vision started to clear and I could see hazy lights, red and blue. When I could finally see, I couldn't believe my eyes. There was the wreck of my car, mangled beyond belief, half under the back of the truck, but it was *below me!* I couldn't make any sense of it at first, and then I realized that I was up in the air. I looked down at my body – it all seemed to be there, but just hanging in the air, and slightly transparent. Yet, down below I could see myself, my real self, being loaded onto a stretcher. My body down there was covered in blood, and by the way the paramedics were behaving, it was obvious I was dead, or almost.

I blinked and shook my head, what was going on? Was I dead, down there? Was that me? Or was I alive, but floating?

While my fuddled mind tried to grasp the situation, I was totally shocked to feel a heavy hand suddenly clamp onto my shoulder, none too gently. Someone else was floating behind me! I glanced back, eyes wide, to see a figure made entirely from white light. There was the impression that the figure was male, and his voice, when he spoke, definitely was. "Look what you've done now!" he said, quite angrily. "This wasn't meant to happen! Come with me!"

I really had no alternative as I was grabbed as if I weighed nothing (which I probably did at that point), and hauled body through the air so fast I couldn't follow where I was going.

Down below we flashed over the top of flashing lights, which I imagine was the ambulance rushing my remains to the hospital. The next thing I knew I could see the hospital below as we slowed to a stop. Then whoosh, we hurtled right at the building. I shut my eyes just before we hit, but there was no impact. I opened my eyes to see that I was just below the ceiling of a hospital corridor, and below me was a gurney with my body on it. Gathered around the gurney were a doctor and a couple of nurses. The doctor straightened up, "Time of death...." He started to say.

I felt a big shove and gasped for breath as flesh closed over me as I was thrust back into my body.

I opened my eyes and the doctor drew back in shock for a second, "My God, he's alive!" The next half hour was a flurry of activity, as tubes were inserted, X-rays were taken, and I was moved to surgery for some emergency repairs. As the anesthetic was injected, I wondered if I would wake ever up again, and if I did, where I'd be.

I needn't have worried. When I woke up I was in a bed with clean sheets, monitors attached and a nurse gazing down at me.

From that day on I've often wondered where I would have found myself if that being hadn't intervened. The way I was running my life, I don't think it would have been Heaven! So I've changed. I've realized that there must be something special I'm here to do, or I wouldn't have been saved. I won't waste my life any more.

*It just goes to show you that when it's not your time, it's just not.
This turned out to be a good experience for Steve, because it certainly
turned his life around as well as saving it.*

*

Over The Rainbow

Janine Perrin

I was only ten years old when I drowned. I'm thirty-two now, so
you can tell death didn't last with me. As long as I live I'll never
forget that day, or the land that waits for me 'over the rainbow'.

It started out as a really lovely day. We were having a
wonderful summer that year, or maybe that's just the way
children always remember their summers. I know they never
seem that great now. The days used to go on forever, and I
thought they'd never end, but on this particular day they almost
ended for good.

We lived in Norfolk, a flattish landscape in East Anglia, full of
wide, fast, deep and dangerous rivers. I knew that many people
had fallen from boats and drowned, and ever since I was old
enough to understand, I'd been warned to stay away from them.
But I suppose when you live with something potentially
dangerous for long enough you become blasé about it, and forget
that the danger is very real.

I was messing about, just dropping sticks into the water and
watching them whirl away. Mum and Dad were lying on the
picnic blanket, relaxing. I guess they trusted me not to me stupid.
But I was. I got closer to the edge, racing my sticks, running along
to see if I could catch up with them. There was a hedge between
me and my parents, which is why they didn't see what I was up
to until it was too late. The soil at the edge of the bank suddenly

gave way, and just like that, in a spilt second, my game turned into a battle to survive. I don't think I even made much of a splash, slithering down the mud and sliding under the water, with grace that would have pleased an Olympic diver. It was so sudden, so unbelievable and unexpected, that I never even screamed.

The water closed over my head, murky and green, and I sank. It was so cold it stopped my breath. The current caught my legs and I was tumbled end over end. A couple of times my head broke the surface as I struggled to live, but all I had time for was to gulp down a mouthful of air, there was never enough time to let me yell for help.

I'm told that Mum and Dad realized quite quickly what had happened, and were screaming and yelling for help as they ran along the bank, just as I had done seconds before, trying to see where I was. Dad was apparently throwing off his shoes and ready to dive in, but they couldn't see me at all. Many would-be rescuers had drowned in this stretch of river, trying to save someone else. It was a fool's errand.

In the meantime, my lights were going out and I started to swallow water. The weeds that caked the bottom of the river twisted this way and that in the current below me. It was peaceful, watching them. I rolled over and over, lazily, and then I realized I was rising up, out of the water. I could see my parents. Mum had dropped to her knees, sobbing, Dad was teetering on the brink of diving in, even though he obviously couldn't see me. He was crying out my name.

Then all around me the scene changed. Everything slowed down and all around me were the most beautiful lights. They were multi-colored like Christmas tree fairy lights and they formed into a bridge shape. I rose up higher and crossed over the top of them. Ahead of me I could see the most beautiful landscape. It was quite unlike the normal Norfolk countryside. There were pretty snow-capped mountains in the distance, wide slopes leading up the sides of green hills in front of them. Meadows stretched out, full of wild flowers in front of me. There were lakes and trees and it was warm and inviting. I loved it!

Then I suddenly felt like I'd been thrown into a bath of ice water, and I screamed in shock. "She's breathing!" I heard someone yell, and I realized I was. I was banged hard into something and then dragged down. I opened my eyes, and saw that I was on the deck of a boat, having been dragged out of the water and over the side of the boat, by a holidaymaker. I could hear my Mum and Dad screaming from the bank, and then the boat's engine roared and it heaved through the water. A blanket covered me, and I needed it because I was freezing cold.

Since that day, even while I was in my parents' arms and they hugged me as if they'd never let me go, I've dreamed of the land I saw 'over the rainbow'. The colors there were so much brighter than they are here. This world seems drab by comparison. I feel happy and secure in the knowledge that one day I'll be back there, and this time I'll stay.

I thought this was a wonderful story to finish on. This child was blessed, because no mater how trying her life may become, she knows that one day things will be perfect. She knows that there is no such thing as death. It's merely an opening door.

I have so enjoyed interviewing my contributors and I hope I've managed to convey the magic in their voices as they recalled their experiences.

Afterword

My Own Experiences

Nobody knows what it's like to lose their Mum, until it happens to them. They think they can anticipate the awful disconnected feeling that overwhelms you, but it's not possible.

A lot of people don't get on very well with their mothers, but mine was my very best friend. She believed in ghosts, as I did, a theory that was pooh-poohed by the rest of the family as fantasy. Mum's greatest wish was to see or hear a ghost.

I would go to her with any problem and she would always be on my side. She was great fun too, and we never realized until she was gone how dreadfully empty Christmas was going to be without her. Your Mum, if you're lucky like me, is the hub, the anchor of the family, and without her things can seem pretty pointless.

The first time I had an inkling that Mum wasn't immortal, as I guess I'd thought she was, was not long after her sister Sadie, died. It was sudden and Mum was devastated. She told me one day of a dream she'd had the night before. She had dreamed that she woke up to find Sadie standing by her bedside. Mum had been ecstatic to see her, and May had asked her, "Do you want to come and be with me?" My heart missed a beat until Mum told me she had answered, "No, not yet," but she said she had seriously considered it when she first asked.

Mum had a dreadful premonition that she'd confided in me ever since I was a small child, and it really scared me. She told me that she had absolutely no doubt that one day she would get breast cancer. I don't know if she did sense something, or if it was a self-fulfilling prophesy, but one awful day when she was 69, she came and told me she had been right. She had found a lump and it had been diagnosed as fast growing cancer.

The whole family was terrified, but positive, and Mum was strong. Sure enough, after surgery and arduous radiation therapy, she was given a provisional 'all clear', and we all breathed again.

Five years later, and we were celebrating. It wasn't coming back, and Mum was safe. It was over, we thought. But it wasn't.

A few weeks later Mum had a stroke, and me and my husband Tony, rushed from our home in Norfolk to a London hospital, where she had been taken, fearing the worst. Mum was tiny – just over five foot, but yet again, her great strength pulled her through, and she soon recovered from the confusion the stroke had caused her temporarily.

However, the cause of the stroke was a greater worry. It seemed that the radiation therapy, which today has so much greater accuracy, had been too strong five years previously. It had burned and permanently damaged the tissue, including the veins and arteries. This had left Mum with a weakness in that area, just under her arm, and that had clogged up, causing the stroke. There could be more problems, unless surgery could clear it. Tony and I waited anxiously with my Dad for the surgeon to come and tell us what he had been able to do. When he did he was cautiously happy with the results. He had repaired the vein and told us that only time would tell if it would hold. We went home full of hope. Then a few days later we got a dreadful phone call. Mum had hemorrhaged and she had been put on a ventilator. Her heart was showing signs of strain and we should return to the hospital immediately. Nobody needed to spell out that they expected her to die.

That journey down the motorway was hell. I was managing to keep it all together when the song, *'Please Don't Go'*, came on the radio. KC and The Sunshine Band sang, *"So please don't go, don't go, don't go away, please don't go, don't go, I'm begging you to stay. If you live, at least in my life time I had one dream come true I was blessed to be loved by someone as wonderful as you."*

I found myself using it as a prayer, tears streaming down my face. We left the car parked in the road, risking it being towed away, and flew into the hospital foyer. There was my Dad, and I fell into his arms, sobbing, "Is she…?"

"She's all right," said Dad, "She rallied!" His face lit up in a smile of pure joy, mirroring my own.

A week later things seemed to have stabilized. It was a Friday night and Tony and I went to bed early so that we'd be up at the crack of dawn to see to all our animals before driving down to London to see Mum. With luck we would be told she could go home, where Dad was desperate to start looking after her.

But we were woken at midnight by the phone ringing. Mum was back in surgery, and she would be in intensive care in the morning. I wanted to leave right then, but Dad, not wanting us to drive too fast while we were tired, said no, leave it till morning. I think he knew in his heart that the three hours it would take us to get there would be too long.

I actually managed to fall asleep again, as I felt quite positive, but at 2am the phone rang with the call no-one should ever have to get, "Your Mum is gone."

I was full of disbelief. It couldn't be true. I'd been asleep for goodness sake! "My Mum would not have left me like that, without a sign." That was all I kept saying to Tony as we bundled into the car in the cold, frosty, night air.

Thank goodness I had Tony, because I could never have driven. My eyes just kept over-flowing, but bigger than grief was my sense of disbelief. She wouldn't have, couldn't have, just gone like that. It was impossible. My Mum, my best friend, would have found a way to tell me.

I turned to Tony in the car and said what I was feeling, "I just don't believe it! Mum wouldn't have done this. She would have sent me a sign…"

"Oh my God," Tony breathed, "Look…." He was pointing up

the road, and there slowing descending through the atmosphere was a bright, white light, a shooting star, a meteor. It passed across the road ahead, directly in front of us as we drove towards it, and at the same time an overpowering scent of freesias filled the car. Freesias, my Mum's favourite perfume, her favourite flower, and the one thing I would associate with her the most strongly.

We stopped the car and sat there, both crying, and yet uplifted all at once.

Of course we had to go through the usual process of funeral and grief, but any time it felt too much to bear, I would remember that shooting star, and the smell of flowers, and feel that Mum was still watching over me. Through the following months I would occasionally go out into the field at the back of our house and stare up at the night sky, challenging Mum to prove it again. Every single time, a star would flare across the heavens. Or I would sit and think of her and the scent of freesias would envelop me, like a mother's arms.

It all stopped a couple of years later, when Mum had her best joke with me. I was walking into the hairdressers. Driving in I had been tussling over some family problems, and I had been wondering, what would Mum have done? I was lost in thought, picturing my Mum, remembering the good times as you do when grief eases. I thought about a day on the Norfolk Broads when Mum and I had been unable to stop laughing, getting weak with it, as Tony and I tried to boost her up onto the flat roof of the boat. I was thinking about how she had always wanted to experience a ghostly event, but had never managed it. I smiled, thinking maybe she could *be* one herself if she really wanted to, my Mum the ghost…

I pushed open the salon door. Crash! Everyone in the room jumped as a picture poster fell from the left hand end wall, clattering onto the floor. We all stared at the wall, because the big picture hook was still clearly visible. There was no way the picture could have fallen by itself without being lifted off the hook. Crash! A picture at the opposite end of the room did exactly the same thing. The stylist put a hand to her heart, "Oh my God," she said, "A ghost!" No one understood why I was laughing.

I was traveling across England to Norwich from Somerset, to take part in a TV program called *Sunday Morning*. Given that I'd done several TV shows by then talking about my past life experience, I knew enough to be aware that this was going to be a tricky one.

On the train I felt the need to meditate, and I went into one of the deepest trances I'd ever experienced. I could literally feel my vibration increasing, leaving the train far behind in another reality. I could still hear the sound of the train in a peripheral sort of way, but it really didn't exist in the same plane as me, and if it had suddenly caught fire I could well have been impervious to the knowledge.

All of a sudden I found myself in a 'presence'. At the time I had no idea what it was. I had an impression of vast golden light towering above me. I felt an overwhelming tidal surge wash over me – a love so deep, that it transcended human love by a magnitude. This love was given and reciprocated on an equal footing.

It's very hard to describe the whole gamut of emotion and feelings that flooded through me. It can only be understood when it's experienced. It is overwhelming, and makes it very clear in a second, that all we know and hold dear of this physical world is as unimportant in reality as a grain of dust in the vastness of the Universe.

The feeling was almost like a dog and master, it terms of devotion, but with absolutely no subservience at all. The love and the obligation was given and received in total equality. I felt divine, and yet at the same time I was like a child wanting to please a parent. Not because I felt I had to or out of duty, but because pleasing the parent would fill me with joy and double my own happiness.

I was shown a scenario by this Being. It contained three paths: one central path and two smaller ones running parallel with it. The side paths were my first book, *Ripples*, and my connection to a past life soul mate (whom I had not met at that point, although I have done by now) Garth Brooks. The central path showed a person (who could have been me) being given the role of 'seed planter'. This person would set seeds in people, while sharing her story with millions all over America. I was shown that this person would be attacked at times, maybe even physically, and might eventually have to live in a protected environment. The Being paused, while I considered what I was patently being offered.

Instinctively, without any hesitation at all, I said, "Let me! Let me!" I was desperate and determined to be given the task of seed planter. I would have done whatever I had been asked. Making this being happy was the very same thing that would make me happy. The Being said, "OK" – just that. It was simple, but it was binding. I only found out later that I had made a contract with an angel.

Needless to say, when it came to the interview, the answers, as always, were there.

I was placed firmly on my pathway, and I've been on it ever since. Every time things seem to slow down, a new tool emerges, and off I go again. Like I said, knowing why you're here and walking with purpose in the direction you know unshakably is right, is essential to well-being.

Nowadays I sometimes get answers to questions that haven't been asked, while I'm meditating, and I have the certain knowledge that the question will be asked some day, and that I will be ready with the answer to it when it does.

So, I'd found my role, my aim in life. I became a designated seed-planter. I did not have to exclusively plant the seed of reincarnation and karma, but any tiny seed of awareness. Awareness that the material world we struggle in is not the be all and end all some people think it is. That there are more important things to worry about than having the best car, best house; best furniture, the things that some people concentrate their whole lives on. That violence is not glamorous, it is dirty and horrendous. That on the day we die, we will need spiritual prosperity and that being the wealthiest person on the planet in terms of money will mean absolutely nothing at all, and will do nothing to help us.

Having this purpose in life over-rides everything – hope, fear, everything. It's something I can always come back to and ground myself with, as is that angelic visitation. Just to remember the power of the love-force I felt, is enough to bring me back to my center.

So afterwards I pondered on the 'contract' I'd made and wondered how it could be possible for one person to share their story with millions of Americans. It's often the way – we feel the need to ask 'how?' Well of course I now know 'how'.

I would imagine that speaking on 350 or more radio stations across the USA would reach millions of people, and of course by now I've written dozens of articles for on-line and print magazines too. As for the 'being attacked', well, I've had my fair share of that. It amazes me how challenged some people feel when confronted with someone who believes in reincarnation. However, thus far it has not been physical…

A lot of people tell me I'm brave to have stood up to be counted. I don't see that at all. Bravery is being afraid and still acting. In my case I had no fear at all. I was compelled to speak up, so bravery didn't come into it. It was only after I was well on my way that I realized what I was doing could prove dangerous.

A lot of people also call me 'lucky'. I don't see that either. We make our own luck by watching for signs and following them, by raising our vibration with meditation and asking for what we want. It amazes me that people can't be bothered to do that.

It must be very frustrating for angels who are trying to

communicate, but just can't slow their vibration down enough to get through. They are there – just ask.

Once you understand the path they want you to walk, then it makes sense that they are going to help you succeed. Another important thing is to show willing. Once you think you know what you're meant to do, take a tiny baby step in that direction, and if you are right – doors will open.

*

So, we come to the end of our journey into the supernatural. It pains me to see so many accounts of scary, spooky ghosts and experiences that lead the general public to shy away from the paranormal.

In truth, of course, the whole world needs to embrace its spirituality, not be afraid of it. So I hope this journey has touched the skeptics and reassured the faint-hearted, that the world of spirit and us eventually joining it is nothing to be afraid of, and should be looked upon as a fabulous adventure!

About the Author

Jenny Smedley is a past life consultant, aura reader and author of several books including *Souls Don't Lie* – when Jenny was regressed into her past life as Madeleine (1622-1640) the session was interrupted by her Past Life Angel, and she remained partially trapped in the past and this connection meant she is able to give past life readings.

Past Life Angels, The Tree That Talked, Pets Have Souls Too, and *How To Be Happy: Finding a Future in Your Past* – this book shows how to access your happiness by discovering your complete evolution over many lifetimes. Past lives can be recalled and healed so that we can remember what we came here to do.

Acknowledgements, Further Reading and Contributors' Contacts for Further Information

Jane Amber - **www.Janeamber.co.uk**

Jane is a psychic, medium and inspirational spiritual teacher, whose aim is to help prove the existence of life after death.

Susie Anthony - www.psalifemastery.com

PSALM: learn how to unlock the mysteries of the mind, body and spirit, to master your life and actions through daily reflection and insight - letting go of what you no longer need, and how to remember the sacred tools to give your life new meaning and higher purpose.

email: psalifemastery@aol.com

Gwen Byrne's book *Russell* (published privately, available on the website for the Campaign for Philosophical Freedom). This book offers comfort and hope to parents who have lost a child or anyone who has lost a loved one.Gwen has been reunited with her dead son Russell during scores of experiments.

http://www.cfpf.org.uk/recommended/books/byrne/russell.html

Jeane Dutton-Hill - www.homestead.com/askjeane

Jeane is a psychic and parapsychologist and offers paranormal investigations and readings and conections with loved ones who have passed over, from a photograph. She is also a specialist in cemetery photography.

Jacqui Grogan – http://www.edenspirit.co.uk

Jacqui is a visionary artist and distant healer who is guided to paint 'trees of life, love, guidance and knowledge' for others to use as doorways to the inner spirit that can be used as a focal point for achieving one's desires in life and as a reminder of how much they have grown physically, mentally and spiritually, and of all they have achieved. Within these trees are spiritual messages of love and guidance.

Mary Hykel Hunt - http://www.hykelhunt.co.uk/
Mary is able to access information about people psychically through their names. "When I look at a name, I see it as an array of colours and shapes, even textures. As I look at these images, I start to receive information about the person. That information can be day-to-day – When will I sell my house? Will I get that job? Or it can be about more important life issues, such as What's my life purpose?"

Merryn Josie – Merryn comes from a long lineage of psychics and healers; carrying on the Celtic family tradition of four generations.
www.merrynjose.com – www.merliannews.com

Ann Mullen - See the website www.randall-m.com
For Randall's wildlife bird photography of hawks, eagles and pelicans.

Jill Prior's book *One Moment in Time* (published by Apex books, £6.99) is about Jill's spiritual journey to peace. It is available in bookstores or online and from www.soulsenses.co.uk
Margaret Prentice is the author of *Richard, Spirit and I*
(available online from
http://homepage.ntlworld.com/margaret.prentice/)
"Two of my sons are dead, but I know that although I buried them in the ground they are still very much alive and enjoying another world beyond death. Until my time comes to join my loved ones in the spirit world, I have many wonderful messages and incidents of proof from them to assure me that they still have a life of awareness."

Acknowledgements

email: margaret.prentice@ntlworld.com

Josephine Sellers is author of *The Return of Yesterday's People* (Capell Bann publishing). Josephine's autobiographical account of past lives and experiences encompasses stone circles, haunted houses in Dorset and Somerset and communications with energies from other worlds.
http://www.wessexaquarian.co.uk/welcome_to_the_home_page_of.htm

Madeleine Walker is an animal communicator, dog and equine behavioural consultant, past life therapist for animals from dogs to dolphins, and human trauma release and soul retrieval healer. She is the author of *An Exchange of Love* (published by O Books).
www.anexchangeoflove.com

Jenni Wheal - www.anaturaltoolbox.co.uk
Equine behaviour therapist and shiatsu therapist, crystal healer and past life regression therapist.

Jill Wood – astrologer
http://www.radicalpress.co.uk/Horoscopes.html

I'd also like to thank and recommend the following websites or their co-operation:

www.inspiredofspirit.com
http://www.ghostvillage.com/
www.chilling-tales.fsworld.co.uk
http://www.ki-lin.co.uk/

www.yourghoststories.com
http://www.wirenot.net/X/
http://www.ial.goldthread.com

BOOKS

O is a symbol of the world, of oneness and unity. In different cultures it also means the "eye", symbolizing knowledge and insight. We aim to publish books that are accessible, constructive and that challenge accepted opinion, both that of academia and the "moral majority".

Our books are available in all good English language bookstores worldwide. If you don't see the book on the shelves ask the bookstore to order it for you, quoting the ISBN number and title. Alternatively you can order online (all major online retail sites carry our titles) or contact the distributor in the relevant country, listed on the copyright page.

See our website www.o-books.net for a full list of over 400 titles, growing by 100 a year.

And tune in to myspiritradio.com for our book review radio show, hosted by June-Elleni Laine, where you can listen to the authors discussing their books.

MySpiritRadio